ADVANCE PRAISE FOR *ZEN FRAGMENTS*

Zen practitioners around the world will greatly benefit from reading *Zen Fragments* by Rei Ryu Philippe Coupey. I met him sixty years ago in New York. Neither of us had any idea why we were on the earth. He went to Paris and met a monk with a head like a wrecking ball. The ball struck him with tremendous force, and this book describes what happened after that. I'm no Zen master and can't judge the book from that position. Call it a density of spirit, call it whatever you like, but few people are capable of such a self-portrait. Reading it, you will feel that spirit and it will begin to accompany you, like a hungry dog. You won't be able to shake it. —**William Kotzwinkle**, author of many novels, among them *ET the Extraterrestrial.*

Philippe Coupey's conversational elucidations of Zen transform abstract notions into tangibles of the real and messy personal experience into universal insight. Here is the life story of a dance between discipline and freedom, structure and lyricism, experience and wisdom. His theme is useful to us all: an example of how to discover, within the drift and drama of samsara, the Way of the bodhisattva. In short, Coupey turns glimpses into vision and the fragments of a life intensely lived into the Ring of the Way. —**Richard Collins,** Abbot of New Orleans Zen Temple and Stone Nest Zen dojo, Sewanee, Tennessee; author of *No Fear Zen*, editor of *Mushotoku Mind* by Taisen Deshimaru, and translator of *Autobiography of a Zen Monk* (2022).

A powerful read! Powerful in its simplicity, directness and honest expression of the Zen approach to lived reality from a committed long-term practitioner of Soto Zen. Coupey delivers authentic Zen teachings with candor, depth, and a good dose of humor. Essential reading for both the casual, the simply curious, and the seriously committed long-term practitioner. An excellent practice companion. Coupey repeatedly hits the realizational bullseye dead center for the benefit of all beings. —**Seiso Paul Cooper**, Roshi, author: *The Zen Impulse and the Psychoanalytic Encounter*; *Psychoanalysis and Zen Buddhism: A Realizational Perspective; Two Arrows Meeting.*

No one is more qualified than Philippe Coupey to comment on the meaning and significance of Zen practice in our daily lives. Aimed at the modern Western reader, these Zen fragments are deep, direct, and clear. But Philippe does not stop at giving us insights. No, he brings Zen to life and confronts us with our very own questions. He asks, for example, "What brings you to practice?" Do not look for the answers in books, not even this book. Let this book help you cut to the heart of the question at hand, the question of your life here and now. —**Muho Noelke**, former Abbot of Antaiji Sōtō Zen Temple, Osaka, Japan.

Phillipe Coupey is a true original. He expresses the wisdom of the ancient masters in a hard-edged style almost like a pulp crime novel. He makes me think of what Bogart's character in Casablanca would have been like if he'd been a Zen master. He writes in straightforward way that makes Zen accessible to those of us who have no taste for flowery new age-isms or obtuse academic word salads. This book tells it like it is. —**Brad Warner,** author; hardcorezen.com.

Zen Fragments

Teachings and Reflections of a Zen Monk in Paris

PHILIPPE REI RYU COUPEY

COMPILED AND EDITED BY GUYSEIKA

TRANSLATED FROM THE FRENCH BY
MADDIE PARISIO

HOHM PRESS
CHINO VALLEY, ARIZONA

Cover Design: Hohm Press

Interior Design and Layout: Becky Fulker, Kubera Book Design, Prescott, Arizona

Cover Artwork: Serge Agoston

Interior photos: Ted Paczula, Paris-based artist

Library of Congress Control Number: 2024941690

ISBN: 978-1-942493-98-3

eBook: 978-1-942493-99-0

Hohm Press
P.O. Box 4410
Chino Valley, AZ 86323
800-381-2700
http://www.hohmpress.com

This book was printed in the U.S.A. on recycled, acid-free paper using soy ink.

Excerpts of the book *Fragments Zen, Mémoires de chair* by Phillipe Coupey, originally published in French in 2021 by Charles Antoni-L'Originel, ISBN: 979-1091413886, have been included here, translated into English by Richard Collins and Isabel Collins. This material is used with permission of the publisher.

I dedicate this book to my Master Taisen Deshimaru

My thanks go to Maddie Parisio, Jonas Endres and all the others who also collaborated in this work and the notetaking of my teachings.

Thanks to Olivier Tollu and Denis Crozet for their invaluable help in the work with Zen Fragments, and to Isabel and Richard Collins for their gracious and clear English translation.

CONTENTS

FOREWORD

by Yoko Orimo

(Translated from the French by James Furtado)

Above all, what distinguishes this book is its simplicity, clarity, and coherence of style. Throughout its 46 chapters anchored in our daily lives, modern and worldly lives, Philippe Coupey sets out the fundamental concepts of Buddhism in a wholly different atmosphere than that of the traditional Zen monastery. Originally from the United States and a direct disciple of Deshimaru, this Zen master's teaching is anything but bookish. Straightaway readers feel that everything said in this deep and practical book is founded on actual experience and Philippe Coupey's long years of practice.

Best to let the Zen master himself speak and take note of outstanding points. What impresses me most is the freedom and suppleness in Philippe Coupey's very modern conception of practice: "Practicing zazen, he says, is a lifelong affair. We practice all the time, quietly, simply. If one can't sit because one is too old, then one sits in a chair. (. . .) Because the true posture has no appearance, no form; you can't even get attached to it. There's nothing to attach to." Yet, this freedom in sitting that the master recommends has nothing to do with neglecting the body, the pillar of Zen. Well to the contrary, Philippe affirms forcefully: Zen is not mind understanding but body-understanding (. . .) Not thinking, not philosophy, but the body. Not my body but *the* body, the body that neither is born nor dies, the body of Buddha.

The sangha (the community of disciples) is also at the forefront of his teaching since it is thanks to the collective and fraternal dimension of the sangha that disciples can open up to the world: "It is essential to practice together. And if one has awakening, this second person sitting on the zafu becomes the entire world." Instead of the traditional ideal of monastic life, Philippe Coupey proposes a new secular form of the life of disciples: "Even so, it's interesting to notice what people are interested in today. In the end, my impression is that they're interested in zazen but without the structure of Buddhism." Clearly, within the master's mind dwells the desire to free Zen from its old religious framework, and rightfully so: "Buddha is us, not something exterior. (. . .) Because finally, the source does not belong to the past, it doesn't belong to Japan, not to Sôji-ji, nor to Eihei-ji, nor to the Sôto-shû. Not even to Kôdo Sawaki or to Master Deshimaru. Its only existence is in the here and now, in the present. Buddha is not elsewhere. In this way the mind itself is brought to light here. The true avant-garde is this. Preserving the past is this. The tradition is this. Avant-garde without end.

Thus, no need to enter the heart of the mountain to live the Way fully today, is what Philippe Coupey says in this beautifully poetic piece: "In Mahâyâna Buddhism, one doesn't enter the mountain, one is the mountain." Similarly, it is not necessary to escape the noise of the city to practice Zen: "Zazen is not sitting in silence. It's sitting in the sounds, in the movement, in the total movement. Everything is there. All the sounds of the world. Silence is the singing of birds. Silence is the screeching of crickets. Silence is the croaking of frogs. Silence is the wind in the trees (. . .), and here in the words of Hyakujo: "Fleeing noise looking for silence is like throwing out the flour to find the cake."

It's equally important to note the deep friendship that united Deshimaru the master, and Philippe the disciple. Philippe stresses the primary importance of this affinity as the very foundation of the true transmission (*shôden*) of the Way; this relationship of the heart must never be reduced to a simple paper affair: "If we are not linked to a master, he insists, in other words, bound by faith in what is the master's faith, then what will make us practice?" I like the disciple who loves his master, even if he is not perfect and he may have failings. For if the disciple disapproves or does not appreciate his own master, why not leave him, because all spiritual relationships must be founded on freedom and trust? Master Deshimaru for example, while he was a monk in Japan, concluded that he had to leave this country because Zen Buddhism had become "pure formalism" there. "That's why I came to Europe, to plant the seed of true Zen, in other words only zazen, in this brandnewness, this freshness."

Far from any kind of formalism or dogmatism, Philippe Coupey advocates zazen as simply sitting and reminds us: "It is said that one person who practices zazen can change the world." In the face of such a beautiful form of secular spirituality, which in my view presages the future of all spirituality bar none, beyond all denominational lines, I wonder why Philippe Coupey is still attached to the words "monk" and "nun," and why he does not want to go further by abandoning these terms inappropriate to the current lifestyle of Mahayana Buddhists? Of course, zazen should not be confused with Yoga nor with other therapeutic methods and relaxation. The path of the Bodhisattva (an enlightened being) requires the total commitment of life and body and heart, in the service of all living beings beyond the conventional boundaries of the holy and the profane. It is precisely in this sense that I would like to propose to Philippe Coupey a new concept, namely "European Zen as a way of life."[1]

Deshimaru liked being called Sensei, a comprehensive and secular name designating physicians, guides and teachers of all categories from primary school to higher education, but not as Osho or Roshi, Buddhist religious terms designating a great teacher or abbot. It is

---

1 Indeed, this idea did not come from me, but from the late Pierre Hadot, honorary professor at the Collège de France. As a specialist in Hellenistic philosophy, he advocated "Philosophy as a way of life," faced with the fact that professors of philosophy today, for the most part, only teach the history of ideas as a profession without, themselves, being philosophers in the strict sense of the term.

this Deshimaru that answers the question put forward by Philippe, "What is a temple? Sensei told me that a temple is nothing more than a building?"

—Yoko Orimo

Yoko Orimo has a graduate degree in Religious Science from L'Ecole Pratique des Hautes Etudes de Paris. She is the author of the only French translation of the complete *Shobogenzo, Treasury of the True Dharma Eye* by Master Dogen.

INTRODUCTION

Excerpted from *Fragments Zen: Mémoires de chair*

by Philippe Rei Ryu Coupey
Translated by Isabel Collins and Richard Collins

Before crossing the road,
The Buddha waits for the elephants to go by.
Before crossing the street,
The murderer waits for the cars to go by.
Same spirit,
The spirit of the Buddha.

From Heaven to Hell Crossing the Atlantic

Whatever is beneath our feet or over our heads, or beneath the feet of a Zen master or a murderer, we partake of the same reality. And that, in spite of all human reason. The worst murderer is no different. We are all, in the beginning, original nature. We are already enlightened, part of the whole.

Yet things stand out in the visible world. Now cloudy, now clear. The sun breaks through.

Fire burns, wind moves,
Water is moist, earth is hard.
For the eyes, there is color and form,
For the ears, there is sound,
For the nose, smells,
For the tongue, taste.
—Sekito (700-790), *Sandokai*

Men and women cannot be fulfilled without experiencing the sensual world of matter. Still, it is important not to fall into the trap of dualism, not to be duped by dogmas, worries, money, salaries, social masks.

The monk Gensha said to his master Seppo, "I will no longer be abused by others."

He might as well have said: *I will no longer be abused by myself.*

We should not become attached to the many phenomena that trick us. Attachment is the cause of illusions, illusions that can cause madness, suicide.

Each moment of life is a death, and this death brings us back to life. Always. Even if we pay no attention. This is not to say that we always have to be focused on the Gospel Truth. Humans need the flexibility of spirit found in humor, compassion, play, flippancy. If we are too serious, we become heavy, rigid, and to a certain extent, extinct.

I was born in New York to a rich American family. My father was a tough businessman who believed in power and the glory of gold. In the 1920s, he was a real estate giant who built Manhattan skyscrapers.

My mother, not a happy camper in this world, committed suicide when I was eight years old.

I spent the greater part of my youth in private schools in New England and Switzerland.

When I was nine, and consigned to one of these boarding schools, I shared a room with another boy. We were close friends.

One day, his parents invited me to join them at a restaurant. They wanted to know more about my family, my parents. I told them that my mother had killed herself. Their faces turned to grimaces as I told my dismal story. They were horrified.

Maybe I went into too much detail.

My friend's parents knew suffering, but only what affected them, not the suffering of others, and certainly not that of a child not their own!

They never invited me to eat with them again.

The next day, they asked that I be relocated to another room away from their son. Why this rejection?

This began to influence my youth. All of a sudden, I became different. Different because my mother committed suicide. That's why my friend and I were torn apart. So of course I cried. Cried because after losing my mother and being abandoned by my (non-existent) father, I had then lost my best friend as well. After crying (what good was that?), I had to recover entirely on my own from these early separations.

It so happens that there are people who grow old without realizing that the suffering of others exists. I am talking about all those people, and there are many, who do all that is in their power to be the first in line to get to paradise.

"Let the others piss off. Me first."

This is total separation.

The shock of this rejection was so strong that it "followed" me for a long time. I thought I would never get over it until I realized that there is no such thing as separation, it's not possible, even if it seems to be real. It is perhaps for this reason that I place such importance on non-separation.

When I was about thirteen, I saw the film *The Seven Samurai*. The hero left a strong impression on me. He was honest, courageous, and ready to resort to the sword in order to defend the weak and the poor.

I also discovered Dostoevsky, Gogol and all the great English and American authors. These were my aspirations: I wanted to be a samurai and an author of great books, like them. I preferred from afar this life of fantasy and dreams I found in books and movies to the life I led among the haughty rich, here below.

Maybe it was because I knew, deep down inside, that what I saw as a child was not the truth, that this above-ground paradise taught me nothing about my roots.

Later, in the 1960s, I entered St. Lawrence University in Canton, New York. I got a job at a prestigious publishing company, then I dropped everything. I took off with my brother across the deserts and mountains of the West, searching for uranium and gold. I wrote books, short stories, poems, and other works, but none of that was ever published.

To this day I am still a writer, although I no longer search for gold.

I got married and became the father of a little girl. Soon thereafter, my family and I left Manhattan for Paris.

When I left the United States at the end of the 1960s, I left my native country a rich man. Yet before I set foot on French soil I was penniless, left with nothing. Before moving into a Parisian suburb, we even had to sell our car: a real culture shock for Americans.

Here's how it happened. My wife Ellen and I decided to spend some time on Formentera before buying a house in Paris. In our last days in New York, disinherited by my father, I fell back into Wall Street. The Six Days War was truly an economic disaster, but for me it ended up being quite profitable. After some finagling, I put everything into a certain oil company. All of a sudden, the stock exploded! So I continued by betting on the price of uranium and a few other high-yield options, going against the feverish feeling which had taken hold of the trading floors.

When we departed for our new life, I left the money in good hands, those of Ernest, a trusted money-manager. His role was to maintain the quotes until I called him, and then he would resell everything.

On Formentera, there were no phones, no electricity, no toilets, and no running water. It was the opposite of Manhattan with its constant flux of news with the papers, the live stock market updates. On this other island, there wasn't even a paved road. I was the first one there to own a car. I was Mr. Rich Who Owns the Car.

Our daughter Celine was six weeks old, and our family life was prosperous and comfortable. Before leaving New York, I had given

Ernest very clear instructions. I gave him a minimum and a maximum threshold to never pass, precisely specifying in which situations to sell everything. Our minds could rest easy.

And then there was a crash.

Such a crash that the news even made its way to Formentera! Right away I contacted Ernest using the one and only telephone in the village. Such a panic had ensued that he had been unable to do anything. It hit me:

First realization: *Never leave, even for a few days.*

Second realization: *Never trust anyone.*

Thus, when we arrived in Paris, we had nothing. We sublet an apartment which was owned by some friends (we still owe them 2000 francs). At the same time, my daughter almost died; she was suffocating and we had to rush her to the hospital. When I made the director of the hospital aware of my situation (I had neither money nor national health coverage), he looked at me insistently and said, "You are American, and me, I'm a communist." He wanted to communicate the advantages of communism to me.

He went on, "Even though you are a capitalist who is totally opposed to what I represent, you don't have to pay. It's free." I thanked him infinitely. We had nothing, and he had saved my daughter's life. If I had known how to do *gassho* at that time, I would have done it. In Zen, *gassho* is the gesture in which one joins the palms before bending slowly forward. This can mean "hello" or "thank you very much," depending on the context.

After the crash, I had to pick up odd jobs. A thing I was not particularly used to. Around the same time, when I had begun to practice karate, someone told me about a Zen master on the other side of Montparnasse Cemetery. Out of curiosity, I crossed the graveyard to find him.

The first time I arrived in the dojo, I had a strange feeling of deja vu. Then when I was sitting in zazen, I heard this voice behind me that said, "Here, there is nothing to obtain." For me, who had just lost everything, in a world where everything is dependent on money, it was a very powerful thing to hear.

During the brief ceremony that followed zazen, I watched the shaved head of a monk bow down to touch the ground. It was spectacular. His head resembled a wrecking ball, same color, same shape, like the ones used to break down walls. This was Master Deshimaru.

When I saw him for the first time, I had the distinct sensation that I had always been his disciple. Even though I had never seen him before. This pure thing began to resonate in me.

Later, I passed him in the street and he called out to me, "You're American?" This very much interested him. He spoke English, a rough English tinged with a strong Japanese accent. He asked me, "What do you do?" I told him I was a writer.

He was looking for someone to write for him. I was afraid he would ask me to do a lot of work for him, which, as it turned out, he did. He always pushed me past my limits.

Deshimaru was a son of the earth, a child of the world, for whom the fruits always surpassed the promise of the flowers.

In the 1960s, I remember when one group of disciples asked Deshimaru to expel another group of the dojo's disciples. The first group were well-to-do, well-educated, bourgeois businessmen, who were annoyed by the young hash-smoking hippies. Those immature, impertinent, poorly raised rapscallions were of course always getting up to some bullshit.

One day, the "barefoots" sprayed the "suit-and-ties" with water pistols right in the middle of zazen!

Anyway, Deshimaru ended up formally rejecting the demand for expulsion, even though one of the suits offered him lots of money "to support his mission."

What's more, he threw out the businessmen in favor of the hippies, who over the years became great Zen disciples, monks and nuns.

I owe a lot to him. Thanks to Master Deshimaru I found a direction for my life. It is a rare thing for someone to know what direction to take, to follow their highest aspirations. This is not to say that Zen and Deshimaru are the be-all and the end-all in this world; it is just that it is impossible for me to think that I could have followed any other path.

I was ordained a monk and practiced Zen with Master Deshimaru until his death in 1982.

At the beginning of the 1980s, he regularly sent me to *sesshins* in France and Spain. And after his death, I taught in Canada, Switzerland, England, and Germany.

Even today, I consider my practice to be in line with the teaching of Master Deshimaru, but my teaching is not completely that of Deshimaru, for that would be impossible. I simply interpret his vision, through my own lens.

Teachings and Reflections

1. POLITICS

I'm worried about the situation in the modern world, and was saying recently that we are heading towards hell. In fact, you just have to follow the news to see that. So I guess we should ask ourselves: Where are we going? What are our aspirations?

One of the obvious things we do wrong is in the example we set for the world. It is not really the best. But are we, men and women, able to change that? Are we capable?

Generally, the first possibility that comes to mind in terms of action is politics. Politics are absolutely essential on this earth. It is essential that we defend what we feel to be just; otherwise, we can find ourselves pushed where we do not wish to go. If we don't pay attention, we can even die as a result. We have to defend ourselves, face up to things. We have to listen, we have to understand what is happening and how life works.

We are political creatures and we shouldn't run away from that. If one side runs away, then only one political view is left. Then there are no more politics, just another dictatorship.

However, creating politics for the future, having projects to develop in the coming years isn't true politics. Politics is here and now. Our mind. No separation. Politics is living, it is life.

Politics is also the Way. You have to understand that the two go together. If you stop running away saying that politics are bad, you could then bring the mind of non profit into politics.

Darwin[1] says that we function exclusively for our own personal interests: this is fire, this is war . . . This is passion. This is why we who

---

[1] Charles Robert Darwin (12th February 1809 – 19th April 1882), the English naturalist who studied and wrote about the evolution of living species, which revolutionized biology.

are born on this earth, in this universe, must find a way to go beyond Darwin and Darwinism.

Darwin said that we are born with an ego which develops very quickly: "me" before the others. First of all, as a child, we immediately want to satisfy our desires and that begins with the mother's breast. Then, as we become adults, we test our power on others. But with each one out for themselves, what is the result? We kill each other. You see it all the time, you only have to read the newspapers. So we have to go back before our birth and understand that not only are we not alone, but we are also one single organism. We must realize the global interdependence of all existences—humans, animals, plants—and of all humans—Muslims, Jews, Catholics, Buddhists, black, white... Otherwise, there will be a cataclysm. We have laws which attempt to create harmony in the world, but to implant that we need a consciousness greater than the planet. One that will no longer revolve around our personal interests, but with interests beyond that—interests without interest. And finally, a consciousness in which we no longer desire for ourselves, but desire what the universe desires.

2. SUFFERING

"Life is suffering" is the first of the Four Noble Truths[2] of Buddhism.*

There are many kinds of suffering. To be born is already to suffer. Then you get old, you fall sick and you die. And of course you suffer when faced with death. But suffering is before all psychology. It depends upon the way you interpret what happens to you in any given situation. If you are afraid, you suffer. If you are always in doubt, you suffer. If you want money and you don't have any, you suffer. But all of those things are personal views and have nothing to do with reality.

For example, it is common thinking to reject illness. But the normal condition is not necessarily being in a disease-free state: one's normal condition could and probably *will* include being "sick," though not a sickness of the head. On the contrary, however, the *chronic* illness of human beings comes from the head. Being taken in by illusions—that is what we have to heal. This "illusion sickness" is the chronic sickness of all sentient beings. This is the sickness which gives us dualistic thinking; not just that happiness is separate from unhappiness, but also that illness is separate from good health.

That is why you have to come back to earth, back to base, to the concrete; and whenever you are sick you are confronted with the concrete through basic questions about life and death. These are very difficult moments, but they are also great moments. Hakuin* and Bankei,* masters from ancient times, became so sick that they became enlightened thanks precisely to their sickness. Out of sickness

---

* denotes explanation in the Glossary at the end

2 1) Life is dukkha (suffering/frustration). 2) Suffering comes from thirst, endless desires, attachment to ever changing phenomena. 3) There is a cure for suffering. 4) The cure for suffering is the practice of the Noble Eightfold Path (right vision, right decision, right words, right action, right behavior, right effort, right attention, right concentration).

we are able to practice the Way. Sickness and suffering mark the gate of entry, and if there is an exit, they are also the gate of exit.

Suffering is not something useless, at least not for those who know how to use it. I think that for everyone who begins the practice of the Way—the teachings of the Buddha*—arrives at it through the gate of suffering or, one could even say, thanks to suffering. Each one of us, obviously, has a life made up of sufferings, and it's this which brings us to where we are. It is difficult to say, "It's because of that or that or that...which brings us here," but we realize it unconsciously. It is also thanks to suffering that we search for true wisdom. In the beginning of practice, we suffer physically, then afterwards we suffer mentally, and that is the suffering which is a lot more difficult to overcome.

However, it is thanks to this suffering that we can attain the original purpose of the human being . . . and even before the human being, beyond our own pre-history. Sufferings are the seeds of awakening. In fact, at the moment when you stop following your thoughts, who are you? At this moment, who is suffering?

As it says in the *Hannya Shingyo,** for the bodhisattva* who understands, who sees, who grasps *ku** (the emptiness from which all things come)—that is to say, the one who sees that each thing is *ku*—where is suffering? Who suffers?

This is why we must try not to run away from suffering; that will only reinforce it. And obviously we must not be attached to it either, not be too caught up with it. Never forget that suffering is a thought that comes from thought. In this way we can put into practice the Four Noble Truths of Buddha. Here and now

3. DRUGS

We spend our time running away from suffering, running away from ourselves, hiding behind our careers, our romantic adventures, in the satisfaction of our desires, and of course into all sorts of drugs. One can't deny that certain drugs, like hallucinogens, can give us joy, or, as some say, a state of enhanced consciousness. But that doesn't last long, since these "heavens" are only artificial in the end, like Baudelaire would say. When the drugs lose their effect, "the crash is sometimes very difficult."

These types of drugs—I say "these types" because what is there that isn't a drug?—are dangerous for the hypothalamus,* the deep, instinctive brain which is thereby weakened. All those who have used drugs as a practice know this. After taking drugs you quickly become tired, disappointed and sad… And too, there is a great sense of solitude.

This has nothing to do with the practice of meditation. The chemical activity within the hypothalamus during zazen* is very different from the chemical activity which occurs while taking hallucinogens. Since, in contrast to drugs, the practice of zazen brings us back to the normal condition, to the original condition of the human being.

Amongst the intellectuals and marginals in the United States in the 1960s, William Burroughs,[3] Timothy Leary, Richard Alpert (alias Ram Dass) spoke of *The Doors of Perception*[4] and the state of mind of the wise person. These people did not know, or at least did not study the man or woman of the Way. And Burroughs even went so far as to

3 William S. Burroughs, 1914-1997 Very important writer and closely connected to the writers of the Beat Generation.

4 *The Doors of Perception* by Aldous Huxley, 1954. A famous study on the effects of the expansion of the mind thanks to LSD or mescalin, for example.

say that Buddhism was no different from a psychedelic drug[5]—a bit like Marx calling religion the "opium of the people." This is not at all the case.

I was part of that generation and, little by little, as time went on, we went for the drugs used in master-disciple relationships—like the peyote of Castaneda, the hashish of certain Indian gurus… We were ignorant, however, of another mental activity about which we still had no knowledge, with or without chemicals. We had heard about Zen meditation, thanks to Kerouac and others, but we didn't really associate this with a further state of mind, a state of inner revolution. We thought that this sort of meditation was part of the religion of Asian priests.

We wanted to find something, and not just through the satisfaction of our desires. But we never found "the real thing," and a lot of us ended up in prison; the prisons were full of intellectuals at that time.[6] We didn't find the real thing in prison either.

So, what is this real thing anyway? Perhaps it is the Way, enlightenment, love… Each of us has to think about it, decide for ourselves what the real thing is. But how can we do that if we never stop running away from ourselves?

---

5 "Buddha is only for the West to study as history (…) Buddhism frequently amounts to a form of psychic junk (…) I repeat, *Buddhism is not for the West.* We must work out our own solutions." (Burroughs' own italics)

6 Jack Kerouac, 1922-1969. American poet and novelist, a pioneer of the Beat Generation.

TRUE HEALING

Sitting in the ancestral posture of zazen
Back straight,
Legs crossed,
Head pressing the sky,
Knees pressing the earth.

When several of their relatives had fallen gravely ill, certain disciples asked me to touch on the subject of sickness. I had done this regularly, through the years, and was getting tired of always having to find things to say.

Yet memories began to emerge. E. defeated one cancer and his wife immediately contracted another; B.P. was in agony, struck by yet another very violent case of cancer; X.X., seeking purity, had burned himself to death; and Y.Y., abused by her husband, came to be ordained as a nun. So many memories. All these thoughts appeared and disappeared, came and went with the waves of my breathing.

Then at night,
The noise ceased,
Calm returned,
And time itself came to a halt.

There are a hundred of us here in the dojo, an ancient chapel that we are using temporarily. No one moves. No one makes the slightest noise. Our breathing is long and profound. Nothing is left of us but the weight of a flame. And we are plunged anew in our thoughts.

As for sickness, it is not the opposite of good health.

Unlike "Mindfulness," Zen doesn't teach us how to be healthy but guides us in how to deal with sickness. Sickness teaches us how to live in this world. It teaches us to get back on our feet. When we fall, we are One with the earth. Right now, earth is the medicine we need. And if the earth kills the living, it is only to allow life to be reborn.

There are all sorts of maladies, but the most devastating come from dualistic thinking: "this is good, that is not good." This principle of opposition is an illness that affects all human beings. We have known this since the beginning of time, since we believed that demons had horns. Demons are representations of our dualistic thoughts. They torment us, harass us, and finish by turning us away from unity. When I listen to the news, I am frightened. It is always the law of the strongest (or the weakest), always pitting one against the other until it becomes a consuming obsession of the mob. Even though they are well educated, the ones we hear talking all the time, the politicians, tend to look at the world only from the outside. They never see what is on the inside. For some reason we still can't fathom, this doesn't interest them. I say politicians, but none of us is immune.

We must first observe this duality deeply in ourselves. When we listen to someone who has a different point of view than our own, how can we understand them if we don't put ourselves in their place?

Through the realization that our lives exist only from breath to breath, we can transform our dualistic and "demonic" thoughts into awakening, towards unity. This transformation progresses first in the invisible and the unconscious, then integrates into the conscious mind. At last.

When I was young, I read Patanjali, who was acquainted with a tradition that existed well before Buddha. Masters from the most ancient times already came close to this transformation. Another master of this same period said that the sole remedy to this duality could be found in the triangle of fire. Adopting the posture of zazen, we become the triangle, and this fire incinerates duality.

Excerpted from *Fragments Zen: Mémoires de chair* by Philippe Rei Ryu Coupey, translated by Richard Collins and Isabel Collins

4. SHADOWS

We must understand our shadows.[7] And to understand them we must look at our personal history, our own individual karma,* and obviously the illusions which create these shadows.

We are always talking about "compassion." What is that? The compassionate person is, first of all, someone who knows themselves. For example, each one of us confronts our emotions, and especially when they could become passions. Passion creates the seeds of life and death. If we don't make an effort, a real effort, to dissolve our passions, we only do a lot of harm, not just to ourselves and those close to us, but also to everyone else in the world.

Shadows are also repeated mistakes. Everyone makes mistakes, but most people follow their shadows; they hold on to them, nurture them. Here and now we should not develop them, let alone create more of them, but stop them straight away. If you don't stop maintaining these shadows straight away, you'll spend your whole life running around after these same shadows, encouraging and cultivating them, and you'll just end up visiting a psychiatrist for the next ten years or so. Our practice is to cut through these things. Right away. "Harmonize yourself with the sky" Master Dogen* said, "recognize your shadows and erase all trace of them."

Stopping illusions, watching them, and forgetting them, in fact, all happens simultaneously. It's a question of mind. If, for example, during your zazen practice you manage to stop practicing for yourself, in other words you understand that you are practicing *for* the whole world, then these shadows, these emotions, become those of the whole world.

---

7 "Karmic knots," obstructions. Traces of our thoughts.

That is why, in Zen* we repeat, "Let your thoughts go." That's what we are doing in a dojo.* It is entering the coffin, but you could also say that it's entering "heaven." When you enter the dojo you come back to *ku*, the non-substance of all things.

5. WHAT BRINGS YOU TO PRACTICE

The first time I arrived at the Pernety Dojo in 1972, there was a sign on the entrance which said "Soto Zen." I had read a lot about Zen at that time, without having practiced and I wasn't really pleased to see that this was Soto* Zen and not Rinzai.* Why? Because I had read—and thus believed—in the books by Professor Suzuki and Master Hakuin that, while Rinzai Zen was for generals, Soto Zen was for peasants, good-for-nothings, simpletons. However, from the moment I walked through the door, sat down and heard the big bell, this bookish karma, which always engulfs us in categories, came to an immediate end.

The road which takes us on the Way is not neatly defined, visible. Let us take a look at it. We can take note of everything. And maybe we even wonder how we arrived here where we are in the first place? We have all travelled a long road, have all passed through a number of obstacles. Before coming across it—the practice of the Way—many people didn't know that it even existed. And then there were the classic obstacles: family obligations, too much work, not enough money, and the physical obstacles, geographic ones—like the dojo being too far from home... When you finally found somewhere to practice, then the problem of the posture came up: "It hurts too much"...; and the master, "What's he talking about?"

Once all these obstacles have been overcome, new barriers appear, and in the end a lot of people who begin to practice zazen don't continue for very long. That makes us wonder: What it is that motivates one person to really enter into the practice, to come to the dojo often and regularly, to do retreats, attend summer camps, while others do not?

There are all sorts of explanations. Some people, in fact, use the excuse that it's due to financial insecurity, and that it's only with money and free time that one can come and practice.

The Dome of the Sacré-Coeur, Montmartre
"...the great wish, the secret action..."

But this just isn't so. If someone really gets into the practice, it's because of their *kan.** *Kan,* the great vow. Of course, I'm not talking about the vows you make when you want to lose weight, or give up alcohol, drugs or cigarettes, or to go to the swimming pool or, in like mind, come to the dojo every day. I'm not talking about those sorts of vows; they are not important at all. I'm talking about *kan*, something which lasts a long time, a very long time. Not just during one lifetime, but life after life. I'm talking about a profound aspiration—that vow we take which is without goal.

And so, why do people not stay in the practice? Is it because despite everything, they remain forever goal-orientated?

Kan is a decisive action. There is no longer a choice. However, a conscious effort is needed, especially at the beginning of the practice. An effort of the mind. And that is true for everything. If we ignore the importance of effort, the human's evolution stops, and the body, like the mind, degenerates.

Kan is not something you can show to others—even if you are seen coming regularly to the dojo. *Kan* is something hidden. It's the secret action, in the depths of each person's mind. Whatever happens you must keep your *kan*; you must protect it naturally and unconsciously.

To those who continue the practice, we say you should come to the dojo regularly. Come whenever you can and try to come on the same day at the same time. This is a good habit to cultivate. Each person must do their best. But be careful, as habit can quickly become mechanical, and you end up coming to the dojo like you go to the office: you park your car—as you would your body on a *zafu*—then off you go into your thoughts, your dreams... Then you come back an hour later when the bell rings, pay for your parking space at the exit, and leave. And that's when you lose your *kan*, this great vow which motivated you to practice in the first place.

In Buddhism, *kan* is the greatest vow that you can make, the strongest. All monks, all the buddhas and patriarchs have made *kan*. There is a total difference between making a habit out of your practice and making *kan*. A habit generally becomes a desire for personal satisfaction, whereas *kan* becomes our life.

Some scientists put some carp into a pond. This pond had no structure, no middle, no point of focus, and so the carp swam any way they wanted. We could say that, like us, their ego, their personal vision was taking them sometimes here, sometimes there. They swam as the fancy took them, drifting, with their ego following what suited them at the time. The scientists noticed that the carp were not in good shape; they were mistrustful, scrawny, sick and soon died.

In another pond of carp, the scientists placed a rock in the middle. In this way the carp could swim around the rock, all in the same direction. Thanks to this practice of swimming around the rock, these carp became strong, their scales shone and they lived a long time, in any case much longer than those who didn't have this continuous practice.

It is not the individual practice which leads the ego, as in the first case, but the practice of working together. This is not work for self-nourishment, as is often the case with human beings. It is working to be able to realize our *kan*, our ideal, not just for a single life, not just for our own life, but for life after life.

So, you can imagine what importance it can have on the human being if there is, in the middle of your life, a rock like that, like a headlamp, like a magnetic field, like zazen.

6. IN THE SPIRIT OF THE RULES

When you come to a dojo for the first time, perhaps to participate in an introduction, you discover there are a lot of rules to follow. However, it's not really a question of obeying and following the rules externally, but rather about disciplining yourself. That's the beginning of practice. In any case "discipline" has the same root as "disciple." That means, "to learn."

Learning how to move around in the dojo: how to enter, how to sit, how to leave, how to ring the bell… For those who direct zazen, ringing the bell exactly on time is important. For those who practice in the dojo it's the same: enter with your left foot, exit with your right foot, do *gassho*[8]*—not to the altar but in the direction of the altar—do *gassho* before sitting down, and then nothing. You practice *samadhi*,* concentration on no one thing in particular. Then the bell sounds, you chant the sutra,* you do *gassho* and you leave. To have an order in how the dojo functions, and how your everyday life functions as well, is the heart of Buddhism. To function exactly within a given context, like in the context of the dojo, can become your first step in the direction of internal freedom, for you and for us all.

The rules, even though they are generally transitory, support the tradition. You follow the rules here and now. It has been done throughout the centuries and it will be done in the future. That's tradition. A tradition necessitates always being awake and open, and also welcoming. That is to say that the master should always be attentive and know how to create a welcome; but he or she must also be completely single-minded and determined. Otherwise, the lineage will no longer be alive; it will only be good for history, for a museum.

---

8 To bow with the hands joined.

We who practice the Way are just like everyone else. But at the same time, we haven't changed at all over the centuries. In the dojo, still the same kimono, the same color, still the same *kesa*,[9]* which can be either thick wool or fine cotton.

Wearing the robe is a way of breaking ties with your life before, and with who you were. It is also setting an example. New people can wear trousers, that doesn't matter, but it is better not to wear jewelry, make-up, perfume... During ordination, we receive the *kolomo*. That means that we get rid of everything superficial. If we wear the *kolomo*, the kimono, the robe and even if it is only for the duration of a single zazen, so, during *that* zazen we get rid of everything decorative.

The first time that I wore a kimono I did not really feel at ease; it felt a bit like I was wearing a woman's dress. Also, it wasn't practical for the collective work (*samu*), for doing the washing up, etc. But one thing was clear, it made zazen easier, with the foot on the bare thigh, against the skin, and with nothing constraining the circulation in the knees.

When you start to practice you follow a path which is clearly indicated. It's a small path, but it goes straight ahead, and it is not difficult to know where you are going. Some time after Buddha's death the path was given a name. It was called Hinayana.* It is not just a simple and direct path, but it also has great dignity, great nobility.

When all the gestures, all the actions have become natural, you come upon a very big path, much more difficult to follow, since you don't know the limits and you don't know exactly where you are going. You don't even know if you are supposed to go up the path or down. On the small path, you follow the signs which direct you upwards, but on the large path, you go both up and down. You go *up for yourself* and you go *down for others* at the same time. But in order to walk automatically and unconsciously on this great path (Mahayana,* the

---

9 Traditional robe of a Buddhist monk, symbol of the practice and the transmission.

great vehicle and Hinayana meaning the small vehicle), you still have to remain well anchored in its origins, which are Hinayana.

Some people claim that just practicing zazen is not enough, and some think that we have to search for the root of our practice, or that we must deepen this root, not here, elsewhere, in Japan, in the East. But the root of our civilization as human beings—root and tradition—is always *here*. Here, where there is simplicity—there is the root.

And so the sutras that we recite (the *Hannya Shingyo*, the *Dai Shin Darani*,* the *eko** of the Ancestors[10]...) are very simple. They are not supposed to create emotions, to charm, to annoy, or provoke dread. In fact, ceremonies are very simple: hands joined in *gassho*, prostrations (*sanpai**), *Hannya Shingyo*. Nothing to seduce you in any way.

Our practice has nothing to do with formalism, at least I hope not! I'd say that formalism is not something that comes from the heart. In the beginning, when the human mind was not developed as it is today, *sanpai* came naturally. In those days people prostrated before the moon or the sun. When you do *gassho* or *sanpai*, it is the same state of mind: you are one with all things. It is a heart contact. But if you do *sanpai* without this understanding, then it becomes formalism. And that's what *sanpai* has often become. Bit by bit things crystalize and formalism develops. Gestures which were done freely and spontaneously become rigid and conditioned, an action fundamentally cerebral and therefore empty of its true meaning. That which becomes "formalism" is no more than that. It does not help us do more zazen, quite the opposite, in fact.

Through our practice, we return to a prehistoric state, not in the sense of stupidity, crudeness, but in the sense of our original nature, our roots. In fact, we even go back before the human being. *What is your face before the birth of your parents?* And before your grandparents, even before your great grandparents? *What is your face before Adam and Eve?* That is our practice, and there, there is no formalism.

---

10 The term usually used is "patriarchs."

7. A QUESTION OF SPACE

It is said that to practice zazen each person needs one square meter. However, I don't think we even need a square meter. In order to decrease and change our karma, we do not need any place at all.

Generally, we think of space as something spread out before our eyes. But during zazen we do not depend upon our environment, small or large. We do not worry about this question of space, since what is spread out before our eyes is no longer important, only what is spread out in our minds.

There is a term which Master Dogen often used which means "living in the mountains, living in the forest": *sanko*.* To live in the mountains, to live in the forest implies settling into a peaceful place like, for example, in a retreat (*sesshin**). However, *sanko* also means to not be directed by the mountain or the forest, not to be influenced or impregnated by the environment.

This mountain that Master Dogen speaks about is not just a mountain like those you recognize in your everyday life. It is also the posture of Buddha, it is *sesshin*, it is zazen. So, it's all about going into the mountain which is your own mind. The only mountain that really exists is the mountain where you are now. There, where your body is, here and now.

In this vein, Master Deshimaru* asked me one day, "What is a temple?" I replied that a temple is a place where there is a certified abbot and his disciples; a sort of sacred place. Sensei[11]* shook his head and replied that a temple is just a building. I was really happy and I clapped my hands. I certainly had *satori** because this exchange has remained with me to this day. It was really obvious, but I had never

---

11 Teacher, in Japanese. This was how Master Deshimaru was commonly addressed by his disciples.

thought of that. I used to think that there were two kinds of buildings: sacred buildings and non-sacred buildings, meaning worldly and secular.

So, where is true religion, the true practice, these days? Do we have to go to Japan or India?

No need to *go* there, we *are* there. Or to Bodhgaya[12] in order to sit under the Bodhi tree.* I know a lot of Americans do that; there are even trips organized where you can spend a short time sitting under the tree—by paying a lot of money, I guess. That is the mind of the thief. If that isn't stealing I don't know what is. Organized theft as well! The Bodhi tree. . . it is here where we are. It cannot be anywhere else.

You cannot go looking for Buddha in your foot, or for *satori* in your hand, and not talk about mind. "I want to meet the Buddha" is a false understanding of things. Buddha and I are not a duality. There is no separation.

Having said that, everything is possible. Master Dogen and Master Daichi* went to China, for the Buddha, for Eno* and the patriarchs. But what did they come back with? When Master Dogen was asked on his return from China, "What have you brought back with you?" didn't he reply, "Nothing, I have returned with empty hands. There is nothing in Buddhism"?

Zen is not an import-export product.

And so, to cut through this vision which is still very dualistic—that Zen came from Japan—there are a number of exchanges and *koans* like the ones that exist about Bodhidharma in which, for instance, it is said that he never really went to China from India to teach the Way.[13]

"Did Bodhidharma come from the West?" Was that coming from the East/Not coming from the East? Was that going to the West/

---

12 Village situated not far from the bodhi tree under which the Buddha Shakyamuni was enlightened.

13 See: "Did Dogen Go to China?" Study by Steven Heine, *Japanese Journal of Religious Studies*. 2003.

Not going to the West? This means that one should not measure the teaching in terms of East and West. It is a way of expressing our great freedom, in this highly liberating Mahayana teaching. In the end, each of us can only understand the teaching by ourselves. In any case, it is not the teaching that has come from the East or not come from the East; which has come from the West or not come from the West. Don't get lost in the details. Don't stop at the boundaries. There are no boundaries, geographical or otherwise.

THE STRAW-THATCHED HUT

To create the living posture that transcends all eras, that of the past and that of the future. That, that is avant-garde!

It is through intuition that one gets to the truth, here and now, in this very moment. Faith is what is known on the inside, in his bones, in his flesh, in his blood, without any rationality at all.

We can with each moment recover the point of origin, before our birth, after our death. Instead of being disappointed, always going in circles, it is better to view your thoughts from a distance, like spume on the surface of the sea. However, as with seafoam, the depths of the ocean will always be there. And our practice, our connection, our interdependence with human beings, living or dead or not yet born, is located right here in this place on the ocean floor.

Little by little, we can realize the profound unity of all men and women on this Earth—and beyond this Earth. Throughout time, we have always searched for knowledge of where we came from and where we are going: but we don't come from anywhere and we certainly aren't going anywhere, that's for sure. We become united, without separation, and therefore without judgment toward others.

In this square meter, an old man clarifies
forms and their essence.
This bodhisattva of the Great Vehicle
possesses absolute trust.
Ordinary people who don't understand
can't help but ask:
"This hut, will it perish or not?"
Perishable or not,
the original master is present
and resides neither north, nor south
neither east, nor west.

—Sekito (700-790)
Song of the Ten-Foot-Square Grass Hut

When you have already knocked on all the doors
and not one of them was right...
Then at last you discover a small opening,
down below. This one leads to hell.
It's the door to Zen, the only door left.

Excerpted from *Fragments Zen: Mémoires de chair* by Philippe Rei Ryu Coupey, translated by Richard Collins and Isabel Collins

8. THE POSTURE

Zazen is the concentration of Buddha; it's different from sitting in everyday life. It is said that sitting in zazen is *muga*.* *Muga* means non-ego. For those who practice zazen it becomes the Way which disrupts their everyday life. Everyday life becomes the Way and not the other way around.

If you don't want to understand, you don't understand. If you want to understand, you do. I used to have a friend living in Sologne. He wanted me to explain why, when he was sitting with his elbows on the table and a cigar in his mouth, his mind fixed on nothing in particular, it wasn't the same as zazen. There is no direct answer to this question other than perhaps a medical or physiological one.[14] However, I told him that it was important to take up the posture. That first of all, in order to practice zazen, you should have your back straight and he replied, "Well I'm not interested in practicing gymnastics." All right, he didn't want to understand, and it wasn't worth arguing with him. Sitting in daily life is not the same as sitting in zazen at all. It is not the sitting of a dragon. The sitting of a dragon is the sitting of non-thought, of thought/no thought.

Western civilization is based on the mind—people today think too much. That is why the body becomes weak.[15] In our civilization, and more and more elsewhere, there is too much information. That is what makes people lose the true values in their lives. This can often be seen

---

[14] "In the lotus posture, the feet press against each thigh on the zones which contain important acupuncture points corresponding to the liver, bladder and kidneys. In the past the samurai would automatically stimulate these energy centers by the pressure of their thighs against the horse."—Taisen Deshimaru

[15] It must be said that my friend, though by then in his late 60s—he had been an important member of the OAS in Algeria and knew all about Guerrilla and suburban warfare—was still a colossal and healthy giant in both mind and body.

by the head falling forward. When the head inclines forward all the time (in the street, at the office, while reading) the nerves do not follow their normal pathways. We become weakened and the brain gets tired.

Nothing can be simpler than the posture of zazen.

During zazen, the hands are always in the *mudra** of meditation. They are not saying anything. The eyes are focused on nothing in particular, however they are not closed. Habitually, when we are not looking around at other people, or at the view, we may be reading. Sitting in zazen, we are not reading, we are not looking around and this does not bother us. The mouth is closed. We are not eating or smoking or professing some kind of doctrine. And that does not bother us either. The nose is not concerned with what it smells. We smell the incense, but we don't smell it. These things do not change anything for someone sitting in zazen. The feet do not touch the ground, the legs are not supporting the body's weight. We never lose our balance, unless we fall asleep. The sexual organs are completely inactive. The body, like the mind, depends upon nothing at all.

Here are a few extracts describing the posture taken from the *Fukanzazengi** by Master Dogen.

> *At the place where you usually sit, spread out a thick mat and place a cushion upon it. Sit either in the lotus or half-lotus posture. (...) Be sure to loosen your clothes and your belt and arrange them properly.*
>
> *Next place your right hand on your left foot and your left hand on your right hand (with the palms turned upwards); the tips of the thumbs touching.*
>
> *Sit up straight in the correct position of the body, not leaning to the left or the right nor forwards nor backwards.*
>
> *Make sure that your ears are lined up with your shoulders and that your nose is on the same vertical line as your navel.*

Place your tongue forward against the palate; the mouth is closed and the teeth are touching.

Always keep your eyes open and breathe gently through the nose.

When you are in the correct posture, take a deep breath in and out. Swing your body to the right and left and settle into a stable posture.

Old age is often characterized by the slumping of the kidneys. If you stretch them regularly, not just in zazen, not just in *kinhin*,* but all the time, you will have strong hips, and so you will always stay young. In the same way, if you stretch the back of the neck, the chin is automatically tucked in and so it is easier to concentrate. Do not let the waist slump. It is very important to keep the spine straight and stretch it without any excessive effort.

Koshi: Ko is the pelvis, *shi* is the key. The pelvis is the key to the posture. Sitting on a *zafu* (round cushion) enables us to gently tilt the pelvis forward. But not at waist level, below that, well below. Then it becomes easier to press the knees against the ground and to push the sky with the top of the head.

In this posture the abdomen is freed. The breath can become longer and naturally deeper. But for the breath to become long and naturally deep without forcing it, you have to make sure that the mind does not follow anything in particular, that it does not settle on anything.

The breath is very important. It is the link between the awakened body and the awakened mind. The breath is the present moment. What is the present moment if it is not breathing? Breathe, exhale, naturally, unconsciously. If it is not unconscious then, in the end it becomes a utilitarian breath, a breath that we use. Do not *use* it!

I was reading something from an American master who would say you always have to observe the breath, to the point of counting the out-breaths: exhalation one, exhalation two. There is no need to count your exhalations. However, sometimes to calm yourself down at the beginning it is not a bad thing. But it must not become a habit, a method, a technique. What we do in zazen in a dojo is neither a training, a method, nor a technique. How can you have *satori* naturally and unconsciously if you are concentrating on numbers? How can you be beyond thought if you are engrossed in numbers?

Do not take things too literally. Do not be tricked, be free. Open up the path yourself, here and now.

Then, sitting like a mountain, and yet light as a bird, with the thumbs lightly touching, you begin zazen. Zazen, that is: nothing in particular, nothing at all. That is: not thinking, but it is not not-thinking. It is not yourself, it is not other people, it is everything and nothing.

You do not completely close your eyes. It is said that those who close their eyes completely are like the demons in the cave of the black mountain. These are very strong images to simply say that closing your eyes is a way of escaping into your dreams, into your imagination.

It is very easy to close your eyes, since they are, in fact, already three quarters closed. Another quarter and, hey presto! you're in bed! At this moment the body no longer manifests "the precious wind" which Master Unmon* speaks about. With the eyes closed there is no longer a precious wind. This precious wind that you feel in the depths of your awakened body disappears.

I have sometimes heard that you should have a relaxed posture. Natural yes, but relaxed is neither natural nor precise. There should always be a light tension in the muscles. It is through the right tension of the body that clarity of mind and wisdom are brought into being, not through being without tension and slumped.

I had another friend, John Dowie, who did not practice zazen, who told me that he found this precision of posture no help in spiritual contemplation, saying that he could do the same thing, perhaps just as efficiently, sitting in an armchair. I said, "You sit in an armchair, relax, and you won't be able to stop moving around."

"That's not true!" he replied.

"OK, let's try," I said.

He sat in an armchair, with his elbows on the armrests, supporting his face in his hands. And I sat in zazen. One, two, three, go! He really wanted to win, but he soon started to sweat. Being relaxed did not seem to be so effective in the end, so he said, "All right, let's stop!"

On the contrary, I didn't want to stop, I was in zazen. So he went off in search of a beer, and when he came back I was still in zazen. In the end he said: "I say that's incredible! I'd like to do that." And so he became a Zen practitioner and a few years later, a monk.

Sometimes, especially in the beginning, the posture can be difficult to maintain. In the dojo it is possible to move, but we do *gassho* before a move and *gassho* afterwards. Naturally, *gassho* is a gesture of respect towards the people around you, but *gassho* also makes you think: Do I really need to move? The *gassho* afterwards means: OK yes! I just could not maintain it. In Rinzai Zen, if you move, the two practitioners to the left and right of you do *gassho* for you, which makes you feel even less like moving, I think.

Suffering is particularly unpleasant. If you suffer too much, if you are in too much pain, you cannot look at your mind. But that's not such a bad thing. In zazen you cannot escape from yourself, from your pain, as you are often inclined to do. But you can use it! Use your suffering during zazen, use it in your everyday life.

A person without suffering is in a funny state in any case. When I first started, in the first few years, my suffering was so terrible that I was ready for anything to run away from suffering, but not from the practice. And the most efficient and obvious means for diminishing the pain and self-confrontation was to have a continuous practice, every day, sitting legs crossed, facing the wall, even on Mondays when the dojo was closed. I did zazen, not to find the Way, not to please the master, I did zazen so that I would not suffer like a dog, and because I knew that, whatever happened, I was still going to continue the Way. Anyway, this is most important, not to let go of the continuity of practice. Lots of people practice intensely, then stop, then start again, then stop. It is really difficult to continue in such a fashion. So, it is better not to practice too intensely and thus never stop. Just add a little more every day... And then suffering disappears.

Practicing zazen is for life. We practice all the time, gently, simply. If you can no longer practice because you are too old, if you can no longer sit in the lotus or half-lotus, then you can sit in a chair. If you can no longer sit in a chair, then you can practice lying down, preferably on your side, and yet always coming back to the out breath, long and deep.

The posture is not a mold from which everyone can take the same form. Someone who has a problem with his back has a different posture from someone who has a problem with his knee or foot.

On the other hand, if you sit on a chair just because you are afraid of crossing your legs and being in pain, that is not exact, that is not zazen. But if you must sit on a chair you must not worry about sitting on a chair, and do not listen to those who criticize this way of sitting in the dojo. I have on occasion sat in zazen on a chair. Once I had a broken leg, a broken knee. The important thing is to be in the dojo and I was in the dojo. Some elder disciples told me that I was weak because I was on a chair, but it was they themselves who were weak—they could only practice while they were young and in good physical health. Some people, however, come to the dojo even if they have to sit on a chair. That is the transmission.

*Zaso** means posture without attachment. I knew a lot of people who, after Sensei's death, used to say that, for them, the ceremonies and even the oral teaching, was of no importance at all, that it was just the posture which counted. So, when I was *kyosaku** I had a good look at their posture to see if there was anything so fantastic about it. These same people all had *zabutsu* postures (determined, even fixed postures). But in the end, in the years that followed, all these people left the practice. Since the true posture has no appearance, no form, you cannot even get attached to it. It is nothing at all.

9. THE BODY

Zen is not understanding with the mind but understanding with the body. For that reason, the masters of the transmission always spoke about the posture of zazen, the body posture. In the end that is simply what is transmitted today. It is not a thought, it is not a philosophy, but the body. Not *my* body, but *the* body, the body which is not born and does not die. It is what is called *Dharmakaya*,* the body of Buddha. The *ketsumyaku*,* the paper certificate you receive when you are ordained, and which marks out the line of transmission from Buddha down to yourself, represents the blood. The blood—that is the body. That is what is transmitted.

"Whoever teaches a truth which is disconnected from the body," Eno, the sixth patriarch, said, "only teaches an abstract theory." Dogen said that the true realization of the absolute in ourselves is what becomes the experience of the Buddha Way. It is the body which is the absolute in zazen. The activity of zazen is to stretch the spine when it starts to slump; the same for the back of the neck when it starts to lean forward, and for the chin which you keep tucked in. This is the activity of zazen, a great activity in the present moment. It is not something that you produce, or that you understand through the mind, but an activity of the body.

When Master Deshimaru used to speak about the posture, he did not say anything extraordinary. What was extraordinary were the words which came from deep inside him. They were completely alive. One day he was comparing the posture of zazen with the posture of a lion, or the dragon's roar. He expressed it like that and it was completely authentic, not literary. This posture commands the highest respect, he used to say, it is nobler, more respectable than that of an emperor or king.

Through this practice of the body, we discover that we are no different from anyone else—of course there are differences, but it is essential to understand that we are one; and it is through the body that we understand this factor. Differences like left and right for example: the right leg represents *shiki*,* which is the phenomenal world, activity; the left leg represents *ku*, emptiness and the spiritual. These are symbols from ancient times, even before Buddhism, before Hinduism in the Patanjali era, even before that. The same for the hands: right hand, *shiki,* the ego; left hand, *ku,* God. But when you cross your legs in zazen, when you put your hands together in zazen, you don't know which is which. Even though we are two, we are really one in the end. And that is the teaching which comes from the body, not a teaching which comes from the head. That's it, cross your legs! That's how to see that we are not two! To see, to experience, this is religion; it is the experience lived through time, here and now.

For all that, it does not mean that we should identify ourselves with our bodies. Otherwise, we might end up thinking that we are just this body. But as I was saying in the beginning, it is through this body that we discover *dharmakaya. Dharmakaya* is a complex concept, but simply described you could say "the body of Buddha" or "cosmic body." It is in this body that we live. When we live in this body, we can understand Zen sayings like "no death, no birth." This is not a philosophy; it is simply an indication of what we do in zazen.

CITY PRACTICE

The alarm rings twice and I rise up naturally before the third ring, and without thinking too much I turn on the heat, take up the razor, square myself in front of the mirror and shave.

The washed-out sky above, the wet pavement below, the closed cafe, the cold cemetery, the old trees sticking out over its walls, the sooty chimneys, the yellowish light of streetlamps, the black pharmacy window, the squatters' ruins...

And now we are in the dressing room and there are many of us this morning yet we remove our clothes without much pushing and replace them with the white kimono from Japan, the black kolomo from China, and the kesa from the Buddha in India, then with the oldest skin on top and the newest beneath, that is our underwear, we walk barefoot under the sky, over the pavement, under the little windbell in the doorway and into the dojo where we sit with our legs crossed, soles facing upwards, backbones straight, eyes noses tongues teeth fingers feet and toes all accounted for....[16]

16 From the novel *Horse Medicine* by M.C. Dalley, penname of Philippe Coupey. Revised edition (New Orleans: American Zen Association, 2002), 226.

10. ZAZEN

Zazen is the normal, original condition—the original disposition before any human fabrication. It is the most simple and the highest gesture. This posture, this mind and this breathing during zazen have been transmitted from mind to mind, from buddha to buddha and from patriarch to patriarch.

Zazen means to become intimate with yourself, to really see yourself in depth. To see everything—your life, your previous lives—quickly in a click of the fingers, understanding the direction that we are taking and have taken. To understand your karma—and through zazen, sweep it away. Sweep everything away. Cut off everything. Even those great ambitions. Buddha did not become the head of state, Master Deshimaru did not become a general, even if this is what he aspired to in his youth. Through zazen he went much further: he came down to earth.

Za means to sit, but it also means "the earth"; *zen* means man, woman. "man/woman" represents intellectual functioning. To be intimate with oneself means to enter the earth, enter the sea. Or, according to Master Daichi's words, it's like "throwing yourself between the stars of the Great Bear."

We could speak about a procedure of unconsciously/consciously decreasing ignorance. It is not a question of behavior, but rather of freeing the mind. This cannot be explained—it does not come from any kind of structure, religious or otherwise, it cannot come from on high—it can only come from a personal discovery made by each one of us. And so zazen teaches us how to live in the world, not outside of the world. How to live in the moment and not outside of the moment, not outside of our physical body. It is in our physical body—this human body with all its physical attributes—that we become buddhas. I am repeating myself, but the true transmission is made through the body, not through the mind, not through the frontal brain.

Some erudites and other Zen specialists maintain that most of the great *chan* masters of the past did not practice zazen.[17] In order to support their argument, they would often use the *Platform Sutra** from Eno, the sixth patriarch, since in this *sutra* Eno says that you must not become too attached to zazen. Of course. I'm always saying it myself. But they made out that Eno did not practice zazen at all, nor did most of his disciples, like Nangaku* and Baso.* That view arises from the well-known story about Nangaku polishing a tile: "It is impossible to make a mirror by polishing a tile." In other words, saying that it is impossible to become buddha by sitting in zazen. Also, these intellectuals proclaim that what is really essential to become enlightened is to understand exactly what emptiness (*ku*) is.

We can find texts of authentic Zen masters who practice zazen themselves saying the same thing. They say that most people need the practice because they cannot go forward except with a gradual approach. For them, zazen is a gradual approach, but this is not the teaching of Master Dogen, nor of Kodo Sawaki, nor of Master Deshimaru.*

There are lots of examples which depict the central character of zazen within the practice. Buddha, Bodhidharma, Sekito.* Sekito who was living at the same time as Eno[18] were always sitting in zazen—they have even been mummified in that posture. And then there is Ha-shang,* disciple of one of Eno's disciples, the first monk to have taught the practice in Tibet.[19]

---

17 Thomas Cleary, a most prolific Zen translator in the U.S. (died, 2021), and a well-known specialist and connoisseur on the matter of zazen, writes: "Zen that exaggerates into a meditation cult [zazen]..., is a characteristic deterioration... where [zen] meditation is done ritualistically in random groups according to fixed schedules, it results in obsession, not liberation, [and also zazen meditation] was not the procedure of the masters [of old]." See: Thomas Cleary, *Instant Zen—Waking Up in the Present* (North Atlantic Books, 1994) p. xiii.

18 Sekito (700-790) was Eno's contemporary (638-713) [Editor's note].

19 Ha-shang was a disciple of Kataku Jinne in the 700s who was himself a disciple of Eno. You can find a story about this in *Zen Simply Sitting* by Reiryu Philippe Coupey (Hohm Press, 2006).

Dogen evokes this in depth at the beginning of the *Fukanzazengi*[20] and I think that these intellectuals, whom he criticizes, show a fundamental incomprehension of the practice. *Za* is the sitting practice, and *zen* is the intellectual functioning. So put "the seated intellectual functioning" into true concentration without object, you will have understood the simplest and the highest gesture. This gesture, this act which goes back through the centuries as far as Eno, to Bodhidharma, to Mahakashyapa,* to Buddha and before.

Anyway, the truth cannot be known. Nevertheless, we are always in the process of searching outside ourselves in order to explain our origins and learn where we come from. We construct rockets to examine what is happening in our galaxy. We construct telescopes for the same reason, and yet each day we discover new galaxies, even bigger than the Milky Way. We cannot imagine, we cannot understand, that there is no end to it. We cannot even think about it. And that, I believe, is when zazen comes into the picture.

So, the truth, the understanding, where is it? Surely it is in the body and mind here and now, where it resides. Breathe out deeply without following your thoughts, that's the truth. The breath flows like a river and your mind follows naturally and calmly the movement of the water. You let go of all personal stuff, everything. All that remains is that which is immortal. Don't think about what has passed or what is to come. Don't even think about what is happening now. Because finally we are no longer preoccupied with what is taking place inside our heads. We have to realize that this is just the foam on top of the waves, neither good nor bad. Through the breath, the posture, we are at the bottom of the sea.

During zazen, we come back to all the details of the posture . . . of our posture which we are concerned about here and now, that's all. That

20 See: *Zen Simply Sitting*, commentaries on the *Fukanzazengi* by Reiryu Philippe Coupey, (Hohm Press, 2006).

we cannot manage to stay in the present moment for more than a few minutes is hardly surprising. It is really difficult. But, if you continually apply yourself to the simple effort of coming back to the here and now, that will change your life.

Zazen is not to succeed, it's to do. And so, in this way, zazen is not passive, but activity *par excellence*. On the other hand, thinking, thinking, thinking—following your thoughts is no different from someone parking their car in the garage (at least until the bell rings ending zazen). Following your thoughts is to become passive, and this is no different from sleeping. Stay here, in your body; that is activity.

When you go down the river in a boat, you don't cut off the engine to save on fuel, even if the river is flowing in the direction you want to go, since you don't want to be at the mercy of the current. Instead, you run the engine in such a way that it goes just a little bit faster than the current. This is how you pay attention to your breathing and your mind so that it doesn't lead you all around the place. In Zen that is what we call concentration, *samadhi*.

11. THOUGHTS

If you look at the shore too much you end up thinking that the shore is moving. However, if instead you look at the boat, you will understand that it is the boat which is moving. This image comes from the *Genjokoan*.* That's what zazen is: looking intimately at the boat. The moving riverbank is in fact the moving mind. That is what thoughts are.

We all know what distances us from our breathing. Thoughts. And each one of us knows what kind of thoughts take us furthest away from our breathing. If you really look, you will see how you pursue distraction. Distraction from what? Distraction from yourself, from what is, in yourself, fundamental—like breathing, for example.

We always want to run away from ourselves, run away from death of course, but also run away from our lives. If you think that the in-breath is your life and the out-breath is your death, then you want to run away even more.

Personal thoughts—Fuyo Dokai called them the "dirty work of the mind," "dirty" meaning the thoughts which imprison us, always egocentric, "me, me, me"—distance us from the earth and the sky. If we understand that this earth is not ours, that our lives are not ours, that our ego is not ours, but that we are just guests for a while, then we can understand that our personal thoughts are only a form of theft, the kind of theft that a guest commits when no-one is looking.

However, if you follow your breathing, that does not mean that you have no thoughts. When you follow your breathing your mind clears, but a clear mind does not mean a mind without thoughts. It's just that the thoughts do not behave like distractions, but rather like sparrows flying in the midday sun. That is something that can only be experienced, that can only come from continuous and regular practice.

The question is not to avoid thoughts, but not to become imprisoned by them, not to be passive and therefore dominated by them.

I often say that one thought is normal, two thoughts less so, three... That is not normal, that is a chain of thoughts stuck one behind the other like the carriages on a train. In other words, you are no longer present where you are, and you are only creating karma, complications. On the other hand, three thoughts which are not joined together do not create karma.

If you practice without following your thoughts, you have no shadows. No shadows, no ghosts, since nothing is dragged along with them. Then thoughts are not bad at all; to think is normal just like the foam on the sea is normal. There is the sea, and so there is foam.

Some people hate their thoughts. That is an enormous burden. Just don't consider them, they're not important. Let them go. All the thoughts on this earth have to pass through our heads. Buddha, the earth, the mind, it is all the same thing. Just do not pay any particular attention to what is happening in your head; no more attention than you would give to the ground upon which you walk.

All the time, in dojos every day, "let go, let go"[21] is repeated. In a year you will have heard it said many times: "Let your thoughts go, don't follow your thoughts." Master Deshimaru used to say this constantly, and today the *godos** too, again and again. I think this has not only had an effect on practitioners, but also on people in the street, in the city. Everyone says it now, even psychiatrists, even philosophers. And little by little whole populations will be expounding this simple truth.

To make this work of "letting go" easier, we have the sitting posture, the breath, the ten thousand points of the posture; but we should not get stuck on the posture either. Then we also have the observation of the thoughts; this is how we really begin to practice zazen.

When we speak about observing the thoughts, some people think that means observing the *content* of the thoughts. It is not about that;

---

21 *Laissez passer*, in French.

that is not important at all; that is psychoanalysis. No, here you just simply watch them appear and disappear. Where do they come from, where are they going? So, if you do not entertain a thought, it will no longer appear on its own; no cause, no effect. Master Deshimaru used to say: "Refuse to consider obstacles, scorn them. They have nothing to do with what is. Do not take things so seriously. If a thought arises, do not take any notice of it." That is rigorous, abrupt, it is not New Age, it is not modern, it is not fashionable and never will be fashionable.

The idea is to leave your small mind to make room for universal mind; that means the true mind which is not born and does not die. In this way you learn to understand intuitively that the mind does not live in your head, in your skull. When you walk, or when you go forward in *kinhin*, you walk with the universe. When you sit, you sit with the universe: it's a question of mind. It is not the mind that thinks for 60, 70, 80 years and, after death no longer thinks. Not at all. That is an illusion. I am talking about the mind where even the skull of a dead person preaches the *dharma*.* Since what is death?

12. CONCENTRATION

In books about Zen it is often said that you have to concentrate on one point, but it isn't that. If you concentrate on one point you exclude another. Merely concentrating on the position of the hands is not exact, merely concentrating on the position of the back is not exact, merely concentrating on no-mind is not exact either. If you concentrate on no-mind you will create not just mind, but no-mind as well.

During the natural and unconscious exhalation, you are able to concentrate on everything: the position of the hands, the position of the thumbs, the back, the back of the neck, the chin tucked in, the mouth closed but not clenched, the shoulders relaxed... This is how the bodhisattva Avalokitesvara* was able to concentrate on her one thousand arms at the same time. Being concentrated/not concentrated on the ten thousand points of the posture, the mind, the breathing, not dwelling on anything whatever, even for a second, that is the activity of zazen; that is the Gutei's thumb*; that is the *hossu** that Unmon brandished[22]; that is not being a prisoner of time or space.

This is equally important in everyday life. You should not stare at the moon, otherwise you will not see the fireflies that light up the night. We must not lose ourselves in details or we will be blinded by them.

It is always said, "look at yourself," but that doesn't mean get too fixed on yourself. Do not become obsessed with yourself but, on the contrary, by getting to know yourself, you learn to forget yourself. It does not mean looking with a magnifying glass, staring at the navel; it is not self-examination that we are practicing. It is said that you must concentrate on the *hara*,* but what is the *hara*? It's just an idea. Everything is *hara*.

---

22 Gutei showed his thumb whenever a question was asked, and Unmon brandished his master's baton. Both gestures were meant to cut their disciples' illusions.

13. GOING BEYOND

Thought is not just a single thought, but a series of thoughts. Thought is what follows thought. If nothing follows, then there is no thought. If there is no thought, what is there?

Having no thought, or more precisely no series of thoughts, means having no references, since any thought *refers* to another thought. The thought which has no references is when you stretch the spine or when you have the head straight upon the shoulders, naturally and unconsciously. That is being without reference. It is also what is known as *hishiryo** consciousness. *Hishiryo* consciousness is the secret of Zen, of zazen. *Hi* is negation, or rather "going beyond," *shi* is thought, *ryo* is to measure... no evaluation, no reference.

In Zen we often talk about "following the cosmic order." In order to follow the cosmic order you must have no references.

True mind "has no color," it is invisible, it is without form. Why? Because it does not dwell on anything. It flows and runs like the water in a river. Because the mind is in continual change, you cannot give it a name or even a word that indicates, "here is the mind."

Water, like mind, is everywhere, so it can become clouds, it can become rain, it can become dew, frost, ice, tears. Even pus is only water in the end, and this water is a symbol for *ku,* emptiness.

We cannot understand *hishiryo* consciousness. We cannot understand it through thought. We cannot understand thought with thought, nor non-thought with non-thought. And so an explanation of *hishiryo* is just a finger pointing to the moon.

This can be seen in the story of the two bulls.

Master Tozan* was walking in the mountains when he met, hidden in a cave, an old man with lots of hair, and a huge beard. It was Ryuzan.* (In the era of the Tang dynasty in China, retiring to the mountains to practice zazen or other forms of meditation was much more widespread than it is today.)

"How long have you lived here in these mountains?" Master Tozan asked.

"I have forgotten," replied the old man. "When the leaves become green, it's the summer, when they become yellow and fall, it's winter."

"And why have you lived here for so long?"

"I have to tell you," he replied: "A long time ago I was watching two bulls, covered in mud, fighting; their horns were locked when they fell into the sea. It was at that moment that I retired to the mountains and I have had no news of them since that day.

14. PRACTICE

The masters used to say, and some still say the same today, that there must be a strong internal decision to become accepted as a disciple or simply to get permission to enter a monastery. If you are a tourist, no problem, but if you are a sincere practitioner, you will be left for three days outside the door, whether there be a heat wave or a snowstorm, before you can be accepted. Master Kodo Sawaki* had to go through that when he went to Eihei-ji* a long time ago.

In Master Dogen's *Shobogenzo** there is a passage that says that if we want to realize true happiness, we must not walk the easy way, rather we must take the difficult way. That makes me think of a Zen phrase: It is when you put the bread in the oven that it develops its crust. That also reminds me of a *mondo** (questions and answers) that I had one day on the subject of slugs in which I said: Spiritual training does not mean putting slopes everywhere so that the slugs can crawl up.[23]

In any case, we are the only school/tradition which accepts newcomers into the heart of the practice so quickly. You arrive for your first zazen and you find yourself sitting next to people who have been practicing for ten, twenty or thirty years. I think this mix is an excellent thing. In other dojos, in other lineages, separation! Do not mix the newcomers with the elders, otherwise the elders will be disturbed while the new people will be intimidated.

In our lineage, the newcomers are very important for the elders, because they bring them back to their beginnings. The new practitioners listen, follow the teachings of the practice and don't really have much baggage in their heads like other, more experienced people in the dojo. They don't make comparisons, they are not in competition,

23 See: *Le Zen* by Maurice Cocagnac (Edition Plon, 1996).

they are not jealous. They have no doubts about the necessity of the practice. They don't ask questions like: What is my position in this dojo? In this *sangha*?

But sometimes I see people arriving nonchalantly five seconds before the bell, and I think of my own beginnings. I would never dare to arrive like that! So, in this case, the influence of the elders is important. Personally, when I learned that there was a dojo with a Zen master, it took me at least a week before I decided to go in. I went round and round the place, looking at the people, how they looked when they came out, if they didn't end up in a wheelchair. Were they the type who followed anything at all, so long as there was a master around? Or were they...? Or were they...? When, however, I finally decided to do it, I did not tell anyone, thinking "It's gonna be a disaster, it's better if no one knows." Finally, I said a prayer and I went in. I think that these preliminaries were very important for me.

Like I said before, when you begin, everyone practices Hinayana Buddhism, founded on discipline. Amongst other things it's about the way you behave, how you come to the dojo each morning or each evening. Most people cannot continue with such concerns so they go away. However, here we have a real opportunity to practice true Zen in a city, day after day, drop by drop. And the rock of our ignorance melts away, in the street, in the city. However, zazen is not just practicing every morning, it is also following the teaching, and regularly deepening it. Otherwise, in spite of crossing the legs and sitting facing the wall, if there is no teaching, you do not go more deeply into this question of life and death, and it remains superficial. Why? Because if you do not advance just a little bit, you don't just stagnate, but you go backwards—it is one or the other, it's up to each one of us to choose.

During a period of two or three years of practice you will go through several stages, unconscious stages. First of all, you learn to have a concentrated mind, then unconsciously the mind becomes unified. Then you manage to achieve no-mind. Then, thinking that you have no-mind, you believe that you are completely enlightened, you have everything. Then thinking that you have acquired this, you forget; your continuous and regular practice is put to one side. However, an irregular practice is not a practice. If we don't continue practicing exactly, we end up falling back to the first stage, concentrated mind: you manage to focus easily on what you have to do, you could become, say, a tennis champion, but you have lost the Way without knowing it. You forget that concentration in itself is not a spiritual practice, so you fall into the trap of thinking that everything is thought—or worse, that everything is non-thought. You no longer know what *ku soku ze shiki* means, "non-form becomes form" and vice versa. And the Zen ideal "without object," *mushotoku** becomes something abstract or simply absurd. It seems to me that someone who runs off after a number of years, no longer sees that the mind is greater than our thoughts, and that, in the end, the practice has little to do with our thoughts.

Also, you need to understand that stopping a practice after five or ten years means stopping a teaching for the whole of your life and for all other earthly lives as well. That is a pity...yet, at the same time, those who do not practice any more will probably remember the posture till the end of their lives, this posture which we repeat continually. Not just stretching the spine, but also always having the head straight upon the shoulders wherever they go. And they will know not to let the hands hang loosely, because unconsciously they will remember the importance of the hands and the relationship that exists between the hands and the brain.

Zazen itself is an experience *par excellence*. The experiencing of life and death par excellence. But it takes a long time, a very long time, and sometimes, instead of abandoning, we want to rush ahead and so end up by saying that "zazen alone is not enough." So then we begin to make the ceremonies more and more refined: we do more prostrations, we chant more *sutras*. Half of the elder practitioners become impatient at some time or other. They often question themselves, saying, "I have practiced all these years and I see no result. I have not changed. I am no more profound than before." But that is not true. It is just that our vision has still not deepened when we think like that, and to deepen this vision we have to abandon all ambition. *All* ambition. That does not mean that you stop working or you change the way you work. It is not a question of technique; it's a question of mind.

No ambition. That is great freedom. This teaching has been transmitted even before the Buddha opened his mouth, and even before thought. It is not for nothing that Master Deshimaru used to say continually that you get nothing from zazen. *Maku mozo*: do not have any illusions about this. *Mushotoku* is "with no profit in mind."

I said once that attachment is stealing. You also have to put a stop to this temperament of the thief, thinking that you are going to get something from this practice. Plus, you are wasting your time, because, even if you wanted to steal something from zazen, you couldn't. Some people think they are going to find a cure for their illnesses. Not at all! Go and practice yoga, perhaps you'll find it there. Other people think they are going to find a key phrase that will help them in their daily lives. Not that either! Zazen has nothing to do with obtaining or not obtaining, nor with progression or regression.

We must concentrate on a single object. A single mind. That is the man, the woman of the Way. A single path. Not two, not three. This single thing must last the whole of life, and not just for a time, or from time to time. Otherwise, it is just a story of no importance. But if there is a single thing, this thing can become great. That does not mean that we should spend our lives in the dojo like robots. It means that we must practice all the time, whether we are in the dojo or just by ourselves.

When someone is faced with death, what do they think of as the most important moments of their lives? To have eaten well? To have had some beautiful love affairs? All that is transitory, a breeze, *mujo*, impermanent. Faced with death we remember zazen. So, this time has not been lost, and this moment has been lived completely, totally. Beyond death, beyond birth, beyond your small self and your personal life.

In Zen there is an expression *ji ju yu*. Perhaps this is the main reason why we are compelled to practice, to become a monk or nun. This expression represents the joy that we feel within ourselves when we become intimate with ourselves.

Ji ju yu means to accept, to receive. But to receive for oneself and *only* for oneself. What's more, we can only gather this particular joy I am speaking about when we are alone. No-one else is able to understand it, because others are not me. Others are not us. I am not you and you are not me.

More precisely: *ji* means self, *ju* means to receive and *yu* means the body linked to the cosmos—as it was with Buddha when he was enlightened. *Zanmai* means *samadhi*, or if you like, concentration. *Ji ju yu zanmai** is to understand with your own body, and that happens automatically, naturally during zazen. Whether the personal thoughts are taken away or not, that does not change anything as far as *ji ju yu zanmai* is concerned.

I like the way Kodo Sawaki says: "Make the self, with the self, through the self." In any case no-one can understand this joy which reigns inside of being, inside of our beings when we become intimate with ourselves.

We each have our own vision. It is not the vision of anyone else. It is not the vision of Buddha, it is not the vision of Deshimaru that matters. It is not about conforming to received ideas. It is by individual experience that we can finally see and hear. Hear with the eyes, see with the ears. *Inmo** things as they are.

15. PRACTICING ALONE

I am often asked questions about practicing alone. If we are looking at ourselves while setting ourselves apart from others, we experience a feeling of solitude. It is common to think, "I am not like other people, I am alone." But real solitude is not like that. To walk alone, to be alone, really alone, is to cut off from society, and that does not mean leaving your family or your work. It means that you do not get stuck on anything—not money, nor any person, partner, relation or friend, and obviously not on a position, a grade, honors. Being alone is to really be yourself. Walk with a positive step. Be without fear. It is walking on the great Way. Such a person crosses right through the *ketsumyaku* of the seven buddhas of the past.

If you practice alone because you don't have a dojo near you, or perhaps because you're on a journey, for instance, then that will not create problems. On the other hand, you have to pay particular attention if you practice on your own when all along you have the chance to practice with others. If you do that for a long time, you set yourself apart, you distinguish yourself. You could also say that you make yourself stand out.

Doing zazen and remaining in solitude is a dangerous attitude, and contrary to Mahayana. From Master Deshimaru's time up to today we know a lot of people who practiced intensely but are no longer here now. Little by little these people became isolated. They did not manage to harmonize themselves with the *sangha*, with others, and of course they suffered terribly. They have left. Some have joined the Theravadins since they found methods in this school for alleviating their sufferings. But the bodhisattva does not fall into spiritual excess. There is no escape: neither from suffering, nor from illusions or doubts. Through this practice our ego also becomes the ego of others, and so it is not possible to escape. Practicing with the *sangha*—that is what becomes authentic solitude. The authentic solitude which consists of being in unity with everything.

Seppo* had a lot of disciples, but he had one with whom he always became angry. It was a disciple who had not been ordained a monk, but who practiced both morning and evening. He believed he was different and thought that practicing zazen alone was preferable to practicing with others.

He not only had a problem with the others, but with Seppo as well. He would hit him with his ladle. Seppo used to use a ladle for a *kyosaku*. In the end this disciple left the dojo and went into the mountains where he lived and practiced on his own.

Later, Seppo's *shuso** went to visit this disciple. He no longer had a shaved head and his beard had grown. The *shuso* asked him: "What is the meaning of Bodhidharma's coming to China?"

The disciple answered: "The valley is deep, the ladle is long." That's all. And so the *shuso* went back to the dojo and told Seppo what had happened. "I asked him what was the meaning of Bodhidharma's coming to China and he replied, 'The valley is deep, the ladle is long.'"

Seppo said: "I ought to go and see him." And then he added: "Bring me the razor!" One day in the Spring Seppo left and went to the mountains all alone. But he was not going for pleasure, he was not going for a holiday. He was going for the Way, to see his old disciple.

In Zen stories, when masters and disciples meet, they don't really say. "Hello, how are you? The countryside is beautiful, isn't it?" Of course, they have to be polite, courteous, especially monks and nuns. But the most important thing is the Way. So Seppo said to him without any ado, without even drinking a cup of tea or anything: "I'm going to ask you a question, and if you can answer me, then I won't shave your head; if not, I will shave your head and you will become a monk and receive my ordination." Without waiting, the disciple got up, washed his hair and put his head in front of Seppo. That's all. Seppo shaved him.

In the *Shobogenzo,* Dogen said of this disciple: "In effect he was a true monk. He understood quickly, his whole body followed the practice."

One day I said to Master Deshimaru that I was fed up with continually practicing with everyone in the *sesshins*, that it was enough, and "now I'm going to take a break." He did not say anything at the time, except later in the *kusen** he said: "You can leave, but only if you have *satori*." I was really touched. It is essential to practice together. And if you are awakened, this second person sitting on the *zafu* becomes the whole world. Like that, wherever you are, alone or with others, you are practicing with everyone.

Master Ikkyu* said: "After my death, you can practice alone in the mountains, away from everyone. You can also stay with other people, drink saké, go out with women and remain in society. But those who practice like professional monks after my death, preaching the Buddha and the Dharma, are not my disciples."[24]

---

24 Crazy Clouds, Ikkyu, poem 41 (Albin Michel, 1991).

16. EFFORT

In order to practice, making an effort is certainly necessary, but an effort without goal. Shakyamuni Buddha started what is called "the wheel of *dharma*" in his very first sermon. It is a well-known image or symbol. Since it is said that the wheel of *dharma* always turns, and nothing is missing. But in truth it needs something else, something *is* in fact missing. Our effort in the present moment is missing. Without that there is no wheel, nor any Dharma. In any case we must always do more, especially if we have problems with the Way in our everyday lives, with our co-disciples, with the master, with his or her disciples. With those things, just as with all things we must go further.

Going further means throwing everything away and starting again, each time, each moment, each zazen. Beginning again means not to dwell on anything. That is effort without goal. Obviously, it is not a question of tension, nor of rigidity or severity.

We should not push people too hard. It is the continuity which is important and it need not be too harsh. For example, during the *sesshins*, the retreats, the practitioners need not work more than the allotted hours, and they should even be able to leave early if they need to take a shower or something. The same for our practice. We practice in everyday life, we come to the dojo, it's gentle. It is not like in a monastery, which is hard. But these days that does not work very well, it seems to me. I think that the future lies in the way the dojo works, that is to say that you come throughout your life without missing too many zazen sessions, but doing so gently, gently. Don't become a fanatic, otherwise it won't last very long. The same with the collective work, *samu*; we need to be gentle with the people who do *samu*, make sure that they do it. And if some people want to get out of it, what can we do? Beat them up?

During one of the summer camps at Zen Temple La Gendronnière, there was a most interesting situation, because there weren't any "permanents."[25] Normally it is said that the permanents set a good example of how to do *samu*. So I gathered everyone around and said: "It's the end, we cannot ask the permanents to set an example any more as there aren't any. There are only five or six of us!" Times change, situations change. "Now it is up to you to set an example. We are all looking at you." And I never saw a *samu* so strong.

No, it is not a question of tension, nor of rigidity or severity. I would say it's the opposite; it is light, like a bird taking flight or a butterfly in spring.

Finally, it's a question of faith. It is faith I think which plays the key role in all this. It has nothing to do with the effort you make in order to succeed in life, nothing at all.

25 Practitioners who stay for several sessions of ten days during a summer camp.

17. THE WAY IN DAILY LIFE

Master Hakuin, when speaking of stillness and movement, said that there is nothing more valuable than seeking the Way through mobility.[26] By mobility he meant "in daily life"; how men and women get through their difficulties, through happy events, through politics, through conflicts. How do we evolve outside of the dojo, outside of zazen?

In truth we are greedy, we are seduced by our environment. In the past it was always like that, and today I imagine that it is even worse. We are drawn to the left, to the right. We are tempted by all sorts of attachments, positions, titles, honors... And so, we go non-stop from phenomenon to phenomenon.

The Eiffel Tower
"...straighten your back..."

However, it is curious to notice what people are interested in today. In fact, I get the impression that they are interested in zazen, but without the structure of Buddhism. For example, I read an article which spoke about the adaptation of the Native American Apaches to modern times. One wisdom saying noted that in traffic jams, "You have to straighten your back like a tepee" (which is constructed around a tall, erect center pole), and this passage was accompanied by a photo of a woman in a traffic jam sitting up straight and dignified. Or again, another saying: You have to "change your clothes after work..."; just what we do ourselves when we put on a kimono to go into the dojo. Another suggestion of the Apaches was:

26 "...nothing is more valuable than the search made while in motion," Hakuin, *Me, carrying my kettle in my hand.*

"Throw your troubles in the water!" The newspaper article explained: "Sit down by the Seine, sit up straight like a tepee, watch the direction of the current and throw your difficulties and your angers into the flowing waters."

And so in daily life, just as in zazen, it is always important to hold your head straight. When you are with others, but also when you are on your own, at home. When you are in the toilet or travelling on the underground. Look at the people in the subway—so many have bad postures, curved backs, heads falling forward. Either they are thinking too much, are nodding off, or engrossed in a book, bent over with the book on their laps. For many reasons this makes the brain tired, amongst other things, because the nerves in the spine, the back of the neck and the head are not following their normal route. When the head falls you cannot have the correct tension in the body.

Anyway, there was a study made in the United States about people who are cheated and robbed in the street. The researchers discovered that it always happened to the same type of person, not necessarily women, but people who walked with their heads bent forward, since a head full of thoughts attracts thieves. That's one reason for keeping the head straight.

Whatever else, for a disciple there is no place in daily life which zazen cannot fill. Zazen is not a part of things, it is everything. In the end, zazen is to concentrate on every action of our lives. When we eat, when we sleep, when we lie down—alone or not; it is always the mind of zazen.

There should not be two kinds of behavior, one when you are alone, or rather when you believe you are alone, and another when you are amongst a thousand people. Even if you feel completely alone—even in a dojo full to bursting—it goes without saying that you are never alone. Alone in your bedroom, or on the toilet with the door shut, you realize that there are also a thousand people with you. We have to behave as if we were never alone. There are not two ways to behave, only one.

It is our duty to pay attention. On this subject, Master Deshimaru said time and time again that the disciple should receive this education of attention and exactitude from the master: "Many of my disciples follow this education in the beginning, but later they let it go, or it simply becomes too familiar and they completely forget the mind of attention." So, as much as possible we have to maintain this exactitude. Our attitude in life does not reflect *our* awakening, but *the* awakening. It must express the infinite nature of Buddha.

To Feel Guilty
Is to Be in Thrall to Your Lesser Self

As the keeper of this human body, the one we call "mine," we are responsible for it. Responsible for the energy that circulates or does not circulate. Responsible for our thoughts; whether they are dense and block this circulation or whether they are elevated and accelerate it. These are our thoughts, created by ourselves and only by ourselves, steering us in the right direction. The direction. That direction that leads us to the greatest freedom there is.

A master can only show us the way. After that, it's up to each of us alone to be responsible for our thoughts, our freedom. So at the end of the day, who is the real master?

The master is whoever cuts error at its root.

It is not possible simply to pronounce the ultimate truth, to put it into words. There are no words to describe it. One can only give a few hints.

As much as possible, observe
yourself,
yourself, not others.
Look at who you are.
Follow the rhythm of your breath.
Don't separate yourself from your
breathing.
Pay attention to your inhalation,
inside, and to your exhalation,
outside.
To the extent that you observe
yourself,
to the extent that you pay attention
to your breath,
you can come to know yourself, a
little.

As you immerse yourself in this coming-and-going, in the rhythm of your breathing, it becomes obvious to you what is good and what is bad.

One faces oneself, face to face, without escape.

There is no need to feel guilty. To feel guilty is to be in thrall to your lesser self.

But who are you? Who is "I"?

In the rhythm of the breath, this lesser self can no longer be found to fixate on.

So, we open ourselves. We are One *with all human existence, whether it be young or old, strong or weak, innocent or guilty: no separation, no difference, profoundly, and this, before judgment can arise.*

Therefore, if we are not transparent with others, that is to say transparent with ourselves, we plunge ourselves inevitably into endless complications and errors.

Rather than hiding yourself behind personal justifications, observe that which is hidden in obscurity. From this transpierced darkness can be reborn a new "us."

To go to the depths of this darkness is to eradicate the initial error which reverberates throughout the totality of our actions like a ricochet. It's like a game of dominos, where one piece causes all the others to topple in turn. Attachment is the repetition of error.

Shakyamuni, the historical Buddha, went from fault to fault.

Starting out, he stood on one leg for a year. Then he ate only a single sesame seed and drank only one drop of water per day. In the end, found himself lifeless, almost dead. Thanks to a woman, Sujata, who saved him from his extremism, he survived.

Reflecting, he sat himself under the bodhi tree and looked inside himself. He chose to get to the bottom of this problem, to the foundation of himself, in the darkness.

Buddhism, *butsudo* in Japanese, is the Way of the Buddha. This teaches us to put ourselves in harmony with the sky and the earth, so that the mind might be completely free. The way of Buddha requires a certain sincerity, a simplicity. It implies being responsible for one's actions. This, and love.

When we speak of love, we are obviously not speaking of exclusive love.

It is from love that we come,
before our birth,
before our parents have even met.

Sometimes, we meet people who have come from a very troubled childhood. Although they emerge traumatized, they often manage to transcend this adversity more easily than others who have had a more peaceful childhood but who carry on their shoulders the burden of parental and societal expectations.

They might have grown up in the lap of well-balanced, happy families full of love for the children. But such an upbringing can be so stupid! The overprotection imposed on these children can leave them more traumatized than those who were raised in a nightmare.

It is not a matter of turning your back on your childhood but of rediscovering it, as it really was. Even those who grew up without a mother or father have known very intense, meaningful moments; they too are whole adults, troubled or not. And they too can have good memories. Because the child is no different than the adult. He or she can, just like an adult, be alive where another may not survive.

I don't know why, but this makes me think of *L'Etranger* by Camus. I vividly remember the character of Meursault, who I am sure you know. About to be executed, he has less than three days to live. The priest comes to give him his last rights, but he absolutely refuses them. Not because of any political ideology or preconceived religious principle, but because he is so struck by life, by the blue sky. He knows well enough that the priest considers himself to be alive, completely alive. But to Meursault, the priest is already dead. And he doesn't want to waste his time.

The blue sky is also there for the child growing up in a troubled household. And this child sees it just as clearly as Meursault, because they still have a child's perspective.

So the child doesn't have to flee from memory. Doesn't have to remain a slave to memory, either. In observing oneself, in zazen, all of this passes, drops off.

Then is when the hypothalamus opens up, deploys. The mind is clear, instinctive, the thoughts of the thinking brain no longer arrive to disturb us.

The hypothalamus is a little region of the brain, situated just below the center of the head. In the practice of zazen, we activate this region by slightly tucking in our chin. In this way, the neck and the spinal column straighten supplely, and the breath descends to the lower abdomen. sees it just as clearly as Meursault, because they still have a child's perspective.

So the child doesn't have to flee from memory. Doesn't have to remain a slave to memory, either. In observing oneself, in zazen, all of this passes, drops off.

Then is when the hypothalamus opens up, deploys. The mind is clear, instinctive, the thoughts of the thinking brain no longer arrive to disturb us.

The hypothalamus is a little region of the brain, situated just below the center of the head. In the practice of zazen, we activate this region by slightly tucking in our chin. In this way, the neck and the spinal column straighten supplely, and the breath descends to the lower abdomen.

Excerpted from *Fragments Zen: Mémoires de chair* by Philippe Rei Ryu Coupey, translated by Richard Collins and Isabel Collins

18. *DOSHU*, THE EXPERIENCE OF AWAKENING

*Doshu** means experiencing the infinite nature of Buddha, the Way, through the body, not through the mind. *Doshu*: how we walk on the Way, how we experience our awakening. Everyone must discover that for themselves.

In daily life, the Eightfold Path, which includes right action, is everywhere in our relationships with others. Right action: How to be in the present moment? How to have right behavior? How to have right attention? To be attentive through the smallest action. How to make the right effort? And what does that do for us? How we walk, how we move, how we talk, how we think. That is to say, "think/not think; not think/think." Do not dwell on one thing, do not dwell on anything. And, in this way, we become present with all things. Everything is in us. We should not suppress that; we should be able to welcome everything without dwelling on anything. So *doshu* becomes *genjo*,* the actualization of awakening—that is to say awakening accomplished in the present moment.

Yuyu means that which flows gently, like a river—not like a torrent, not like illusions and war. *Yuyu* is to go gently, like during a summer camp, a retreat or in a dojo. And also in everyday life: coming to the dojo, going to work, going back home every day without interruption. *Yuyu* is to revitalize and perpetuate this life of practice during a retreat into our daily lives. It is this tranquility, this *yuyu* which has emanated from Buddhist practitioners for all time.

When my wife and I separated—actually because I spent too much time in zazen—I found myself living in a small room, and Master Deshimaru said to me: "That's very good. Live small, and that way you will become big." Really small. Really small. I did not even have my own toilet, or even a shower, or even any heating, and at the beginning I had no hot water. I spent thirty years like that. I think our lives are already difficult enough without weighing them down with phenomena like, for example, material ease, so that there is less space for freedom. *Really small, really small*, it is like the minuscule point of a needle becoming vast. Out of a hole the idiot saw Buddha and he was able to climb to the summit of Mount Sumeru.*

All human beings should have a practice on this earth. But not for self-control or self-discipline—taking on *doshu* from this viewpoint is extremely immature. It is like, for example, if I am typing with all my fingers and someone tells me that I should know where to find the J, the G and the M, and that if I don't know their location on the keyboard then I'm making mistakes. This is not true. In any given moment it helps to know where to find the letters J, G and M. But now, since it has become unconscious and automatic, I do not know anymore, and that is even better.

We do not need to learn how to behave; we do not need to study these questions. We know, everyone knows. Obviously we learn correct behavior at home when we are children, as we often follow the example of adults, but afterwards we put that aside. From the moment we sit on a *zafu* and we keep upright, we understand everything automatically; we do not pick our noses or scratch our faces any more. These things are past. The manners from before birth appear before us whether we have been well educated as a child or not.

19. ACTION AND ENERGY

Some people say, "I don't hesitate and then everything I do works out." That is a false idea, once more it points to an assumed separation between myself and my ideas—*me* and *my* non-hesitation. Non-hesitation is not something which takes us to extremes, towards personal choices. Not hesitating is an experience of unity between the body and the mind. *Before* thought, *before* decision. The practice of zazen automatically and unconsciously frees us from all decision-making. It is a way of experiencing here and now. It is confidence in oneself.

We could speak about this subject in terms of occasion or opportunity. This distinction is particularly applicable to the martial arts, however it should not be limited to combat, but extend into everything we do.[27] For example, in the dojo during a *mondo* between master and disciple, it's about seizing the chance. That is something thought cannot do, but only consciousness coming from emptiness, from *ku*. Seizing before the action. The action before the action.

Sometimes we speak of *zanshin** which is the action after the action, the mind that lives on in concentration after the action, after zazen. But the action before the action is different. The master's eyes are aware before the action. They are not wide open looking you straight in the eye, they look without looking. But to grasp that, there has to be an exchange. A doctor once told me that it is quite similar to the relationship between the surgeon and their assistant. When the doctor needs the tweezers or some other surgeon's instrument, they receive them, in hand, before thinking about or asking for it.

---

27 Hakuin: "The most important thing for a samurai is to be resolute," and further, "There is no trace of passion in him, nor of enlightenment." (*Let your hands go*; Hakuin, translated by Shibata.)

That would not be possible if, in that moment, there were thoughts blocking the brain. This is why action is *ki*,* energy.

To break out of this, to free each of us from our handcuffs, there needs to be *ki*. Not just *ki* of activity, but *ki* of means, *ki* of luck, *ki* of opportunity. We have to grab it. However, if you are attached to your thoughts or your principles, the *ki* is attached as well. *Ki* does not come from the brain it comes from the heart. When *ki* is not obstructed, that is the moment to grab your chance.

It is nothing like praying to Buddha or praying to God to have a bit of luck in your life. It is about seizing your *ki* and transforming it into spiritual impetus. The disciple must seize the *ki* of the reality of the teaching, and the master must seize the *ki* of the person who follows him, unconsciously and naturally. Master Deshimaru often used to speak about this: seizing the opportunity like the hen with its chick when the chick is still in the egg. The hen sits on the eggs for thirty days and then, when the moment comes, she taps the egg on the outside; at exactly the same moment the chick does the same from the inside. And the shell breaks. Crack! Broken!

We must also notice how we react to *ki*. There are some people who do not react at all to Mahayana *ki*, but they react to Hinayana *ki*. It is not a question of vitality, as if the Mahayana *ki* had more vitality than the Hinayana. It is more about knowing how you—your organism, your mind—transforms oxygen into human energy. If you invest in a practice, Mahayana, Hinayana or whatever else, *ki* develops and you can really feel the difference. I have had many opportunities to feel the *ki* of Hinayana monks when I was in India. And then there are also the Tibetans . . . that's something else.

In Zen we must be very careful with this question, since the term *ki* is quite often used to describe the style of teaching a master uses with their disciple or disciples. We ought to have quite a precise idea about the *ki* of Bodhidharma. You could say that there is "external *ki*," like that of a king—his image, his crown, his majestic clothes—and then there is the "internal *ki*" of Bodhidharma, without a crown or majestic clothes, without a sword by his side. And then there is "Soto Zen *ki*" which is ours, and "Rinzai Zen *ki*." Someone who studies a bit could also distinguish the difference between Ejo's* *ki* and Hakuin's, for example.

And to end this question of *ki*, the *ki* of zazen will influence you a lot more efficiently inside a dojo. *Joriki** is the energy produced by zazen. If you are sitting next to people who do not move at all, then this *ki* will influence you completely and forever.

The pyramid of the Louvre, from the Guichets du Louvre
"...working exactly in context"

20. THE RING OF THE WAY

With a practice like ours there is no beginning, no end, because there is no goal. We know about goals, there are all sorts. If we practice with a goal, our work, our practice, is nothing more than a movement of the body, a movement to earn one's salary or retirement, a movement to maintain the home. But these movements are not holy movements committed to the abandonment of the ego, to the overcoming of the small self.

The Japanese writer Mishima, one month before he committed hara-kiri on the balcony of the Ministry of Defense in Tokyo, questioned young people, ending with the phrase: "The cause for which you have given your lives is not worth it." I have read him, and I have always been as equally surprised by his great artistic talent as by his misinterpretation of Buddhism, even though he was born in a Buddhist country. He thought that Buddhism was fatalist. However, he made no mistake in asking this question: "What are you doing with your life, is it worth it?" (For Mishima clearly "*not* worth it.")

I do not think that people who practice zazen ask this question. For us, the practice is like throwing a sword into the sky. It is not necessary to cut a hole in the sky, the only important thing is the act of throwing the sword again and again. The metal shines in the sun, beyond thought: this consciousness which shines through the blue sky.

Some masters call this "the perfection of Zen." This perfection, which I would rather call "realization," is never accomplished; it continues. That is *gyoji*.* *Gyo* means "practice" and *ji* means "to continue," also in a sense "to protect." Continue always, without fear of life or death. And learn to die while maintaining dignity, without complaining. That is the way to live.

Even though Mahakashyapa came from an aristocratic family, like Buddha, his life became completely poor, simple. He only ate once a day, he slept on the street—mostly in cemeteries, but also under the trees. He only did zazen. He never slept in a temple, nor in a hermitage, nor even in a tent or a house, but outside, without a mattress, without a blanket. Like a dog. That was his *gyoji*, his *dokan*.* That is extremely important: continuous practice for all human beings. Without continuity, there is no practice. *Dokan: do*, the Way; *kan*, the circle, the ring. Practice without beginning or end. That is immortality, that which is immortal, and which continues. That is what we have received and what we transmit.

21. FORMS AND TRADITION

How can the Way express itself naturally and automatically in our lives? The Way that we follow can only be realized through the mastery of the particular forms of a concrete practice, and naturally of a specific tradition. It is not that one is better than another, it's just that there is only one. It is through the so-called rules, the discipline of a tradition—in other words, through the body and not the brain—that true wisdom can blossom. So, it is out of any one specific form that we discover what is behind this form, behind all forms; that is to say non-form. Through the practice of zazen, the practice of the posture, of Zen, we discover continuous practice, *muso*,* non-posture, the non-aspect of what we are doing and of what is. That is where we find true freedom. Freedom cannot exist outside of the rules.

Freedom, for example, does not mean turning up when you like, usually late. That is not freedom at all; that is unconsciousness, non-concentration, non-observation. And so, all traditions, all religions, have rules. To attain *satori* you have to follow Zen traditions, and to obtain the grace of God you have to follow Christian traditions. It is certainly not any-old-how.

As practitioners, we should not be following everyday life. It is daily life—our daily lives—which follow us, here and now. In any case it is not the rules which come first; it is the event which comes first. In the beginning there are no rules. Then one person arrives late—still no rules. Two people, three, four... Then a rule is made.

If an elder practitioner, a teacher or someone responsible, does not follow the rules, then who will follow them? If you do not follow them, then, when the time comes for you to teach, how will you get anyone to follow you?

The importance of form is incontestable. For example, when two people are talking together, that also becomes a ceremony, which does not mean that it becomes false: through ceremony it becomes profound.

The monks in olden times, in order to speak to each other, would hold their hands flat against the sternum.[28] That is a form of mutual respect. Holding your hands like that means you are less inclined to talk of trivialities. Whatever you do, you should do it as precisely as possible, even though mistakes no longer retain any importance—that is, from the moment you realize that you have made them.

And so, it is not necessary to do impeccable ceremonies in impeccable dress. As much as possible, you need to be refined, but natural. The true school, the only authentic teaching is the one which goes directly to the mind of the Way, not your small mind which wants to be stylish, attractive. It has always been said that Zen is austere, and it is true. It is a practice which does not depend on the appearance of things.

It is essential to remain simple, because people always have a tendency to add more and more. In a way you can understand it. They say that when Buddha was enlightened, he developed marks which distinguished him from other people, signs. He had apparently thirty-two. He had, as you can see on some statues, a protuberance on his head, very long ears and a dot on his forehead between his eyebrows. These signs are necessary perhaps, but we should not become attached to anything, above all not to any one particular aspect, even one particular aspect of Buddha. Buddha is us, not something outside of ourselves. Buddha himself said in one of the *sutras:* "Wherever there is possession of insignia there is fraud. Wherever there is non-possession of non-insignia there is no fraud." That is where our teaching, our practice begins. It begins, not from a god, but from an awakened human being. And Buddha has made this possible for every human being. He also said: "I have arrived at buddhahood and you, all of you, are the buddhas of the future."

For everyone these days who plays, let us say, classical music, there is no complete originality in their work, as we all know Bach,

---

28 That means in *shashu.*

Beethoven, and other great composers. But this work, this music, manifests itself anew each time with a different conductor. The base does not change, but the way of expressing it changes. It is like that for all true creations. In the end, the source does not belong to the past, it does not belong to Japan, neither to *Soji-ji** nor *Eihei-ji* nor to the *Sotoshu.** Nor does it belong to Kodo Sawaki, or Master Deshimaru. It exists only here and now, in the present. Buddha is not anywhere else. This is how mind itself is manifest. That is true avant-garde. That is the preservation of the past. That is tradition, forever avant-garde.

To come back to the essence, that is the true school, that is what has been certified: our minds with no outward show. A master, I believe it was Unmon, said: "Since the birth of Buddha the world has become too complicated, invaded by the *sutras*. You just have to do zazen and receive the *kyosaku*." The *sutras*, special ceremonies, constricting clothes...you only have to do zazen and receive the *kyosaku.*

NO NEED FOR A TEMPLE

I created, with my disciples, the Sangha Sans Demeure (Sangha With No Fixed Abode) in 2001. I encourage them to lead sesshin and to support one another. Of three hundred practitioners, forty have led sesshin in Germany, Switzerland, and France. And this is completely outside the authority of official Buddhism. We have no temple and we have no need of one. Nothing is fixed.

In Zen and in religion in general, one often finds two opposing tendencies. Some are drawn toward ecclesiastical guardianship. Others are drawn towards religious autonomy.

Autonomy is the capacity to decide for oneself and by oneself.

Guardianship, extraordinarily common, imposes an exterior authority, which in exchange protects you in your practice, bestows on you all sorts of titles, always putting you centerstage in your mission.

But "guardianship" has no place in religious autonomy. In the Sangha Sans Demeure, our teaching is to find, for each and every one of us, an autonomy which is ours alone. In the dojo as well as in daily life. The organization of the sangha mirrors and emphasizes this autonomy on the part of the practitioners.

This is not a vision I have chosen over another. If one knows oneself profoundly, one does not choose, one knows, one is, that's all. Thus, conflicts with others are not necessary because those who oppose you haven't chosen their direction any more than you have.

From the outset, then, there should be no problem.

Excerpted from *Fragments Zen: Mémoires de chair* by Philippe Rei Ryu Coupey, translated by Richard Collins and Isabel Collins

22. THE PRECEPTS

Concerning everything in the dojo, it is extremely important to follow the rules exactly, even though the rules can change from one day to the next. Rules, the precepts, or *kai** are neither commandments nor obstacles, they are aspirations. They do not come from the outside; they are not doctrines which are imposed upon us; they come from ourselves. In the end they are not external, but internal: we aspire to evolve, to deepen, to share our enlightenment with others. But to think that we have to follow them: *kai* 1, *kai* 2, *kai* 3..."do not kill"... If you have already killed then you can seriously deepen this *kai*. But if you have never killed...? The *kai* are much more profound when they are seen in their entirety. That is, not to kill with words, not to kill with a look. We must understand the *kai* like that. Not like a prohibition.

Even people who have received ordination are free to do what they like with their lives. They who are ordained follow the *kai*, the precepts, unconsciously and naturally; and that is why the master can say, "Do as you like." It is like, during zazen, we practice all the precepts unconsciously, automatically and naturally. Obviously, we are practicing the five great precepts of the bodhisattva, so we are not engaged in trivial talk, in telling lies to others or to oneself, or in criticism; afterwards or before perhaps, but not during zazen.

When you have understood the practice of the Way, in each moment you follow the *kai* unconsciously and there are no longer any limits. Going to the cafe to look at the women, is that a bad thing?

These *kai* exist because people are fundamentally sick. In the beginning, in Buddha's time, people drank wine. But one day some *bhikshus* were found completely drunk, collapsed in front of the entrance gates to the town where Buddha was living at the time.[29] A number

---

29 *The Historical Buddha*, by H. W. Schumann, (Motilal Benarsidass, 2004).

of people reacted and went to see him saying: "This is no good, it is not a true religion." So Buddha said: "All right, from now on alcohol is forbidden." But on his deathbed Buddha said to Ananda* while taking account of all the precepts: "You can delete them all." After Buddha's death, Mahakashyapa asked Ananda: "Which *kai* shall we delete?" And Ananda started to count them: "This one, that one..." But he couldn't remember them all, so Mahakashyapa said: "Well in that case, we should keep them all."

We have to know how to drink, how to be with a woman or with a man. It is a question of attachment not a question of petty morality. It must not harm you, nor bring harm to others and it must not take you away from the path. This is a very wide point of view, but at the same time, quite precise. Of course, we are not completely ready to live that way today. There is a bar at La Gendronnière and a lot of people outside our *sangha** have been critical of that. However, we have to know how to be strong to continue as we do, keeping an open mind and not falling into restrictions, common concepts imposed from the outside.

There are schools of Zen full of stances about all sorts of things, but the true teaching does not take a stance, neither on what we eat nor on anything else. Zen began with Mahakashyapa's smile when Buddha turned the flower. Where is the stance? Simply not to lose the root.

If you want to eat meat, then eat meat. If you do not want to eat meat, then don't eat it. Like Buddha, when there was nothing else to eat, he ate meat. His monks who were going to Kashmir said: "Look Buddha, there is only meat here." And so he said: "Eat the meat!" Obviously.

Of course it is not necessary to eat meat while on retreat or otherwise. In any case, on a retreat it is better not to eat it because you can get pains in your knees. But you shouldn't stick to this like a doctrine. You should not take the moral high ground: this is good, this is not good. That is not Zen at all.

Good, bad—things are not so simple. For example, one day I was caught stealing. I went home and said to myself: "God! You're a thief!"

I looked around and thought: "There are a lot of things here I have stolen... that's not very good..." And then I realized: "But I have no need of all these things either." So I stopped stealing. I had already been practicing zazen for a long time when I was caught, but I stole because I did not have any money. I stole a steak once in a Monoprix-supermarket. Before that I was working nights at CBS News and some journalists would come into the office late in the evening to steal things; I used to watch them. "OK, they steal, that's how it is." I stole a few things too, some books, paper, sticky tape...then I had this *satori* at the Monoprix. So what happened? I no longer had a place in this job, something wasn't right. Because I was no longer like the others. After that I did not work there anymore and I was reformed. I was no longer a thief.

Once I went to a night club which a friend of mine was directing in Montparnasse. There was some live American Jazz. A woman approached my table and said: "I hear that you are a Zen master." She was a female psychoanalyst, quite high up in her profession. She was interested in Zen, she wanted to practice and thought that it would help her work.

I replied, "Could be."

She told me that what interested her quite a lot—and she thought she would find it in Zen—was morality. My head filled with a phrase Master Deshimaru once shouted at a disciple: "Don't sit on a moralist *zafu*!" And so I said to her, "There is no morality in Zen."

She was really surprised and asked me how long I had been practicing.

"Oh about thirty years."

"With a Japanese master?"

"Yes, yes, a Japanese master."

I did not say anything else. I simply looked at her without smiling, without anything: I didn't have Mahakashyapa's smile, and I certainly didn't have Vimalakirti's* silence of the thunder. All that I could do was raise my glass. Nothing like Unmon brandishing his *kotsu**;

I simply no longer knew what morality was. And then there was the saxophone, the piano...

As I was going out, I was with someone who practiced a little zazen and I said to him: "All right, I'm really stupid. I don't even know what morality is. I just don't know any more." Twenty years ago I could have easily sounded off on this subject. But after all these years of practice it is no longer obvious how to express myself in these things—I do not know the formulas anymore."

"But you follow the precepts, don't you?"

"I don't know," I replied. "I don't even know that anymore."[30]

It was no longer possible to talk about things in a logical, rational and seductive way.

Morality, what is it? How do you talk about it?

I thought about it afterwards and I wondered if religions in general start out with morality, precepts. But you could say that true religion is the one that is found deeply inside of all of us, always in the present moment; that which has no history, and no past. In other words, it begins where morality ends. Then what are these precepts that we all decide to embrace at our ordinations?

Perhaps there are two ways of seeing it. Morality which is quite visible to others, the precepts are visible. This is the external package which, in the end, is nothing more than a way of cultivating one's individuality, one's image. Or, there are the *kai*, the precepts or, in fact, *the* precept which we cannot express, which we cannot even know—this *kai*, which is in our blood, our bones, this is the *kai* that no longer exists since we are beyond it. That is the sound of one hand; that is the *kotsu* brandished in the air; that is Gutei's thumb. If it is more than that, more than the brandished *kotsu*, we are only left with "good/not good." That is all morality becomes.

---

30 See page 61, the passage about typing, in the chapter 18, "*Doshu*, The Experience of Awakening."

A QUESTION ABOUT A CAT

Here is a question put to me by a practitioner during a *sesshin* in Nantes, with my response:

"There are lots of things I have trouble grasping in Buddhism. For example, I might think that I more or less understand something, when in fact I realize I understand none of it. Like yesterday, when I heard you talk about your cat."

"My cat?"

"Because it seemed to me like you were very attached to this cat, and I started to think about the notion of nonattachment. I am using this example to be concrete. That a Zen master can be attached to his cat, that confuses me."

"No one would take care of this cat if I didn't. If not for me, he would die on the spot. When I leave, he howls, he goes crazy because he thinks that I am going to abandon him. I am not going to abandon him: I am as attached as he is. But I am attached to all cats, all of them! No cat displeases me. I think I love my cat, but when he dies I will be content because I will finally be free. I've had him for 21 years. I've lugged him about in my arms for every one of these years. Now, he's so old I can't leave him home alone: I have to bring him to my room at the Gendronnière. He sits in my lap when I lead sesshin. He wakes me up at night. He makes my life difficult. I am waiting for him to die. But when the time comes, I will certainly suffer. So where is this attachment located? It can only be found in nonattachment.

"Deshimaru locked himself in his room for two days to cry over the death of his secretary—it was an accidental death, and a real shock to all of us. I saw Deshimaru cry just as much when he received a letter from his son who told him 'You are not a true master! And I will disown you!'

"A master is only human. He experiences emotions and sentiments, just like everyone else. That is simply Buddhism. Buddha was a man, not a god.

"Attachment. Although we always say, detach, detach yourself, I think it is possible and yet at the same time impossible. You detach yourself, yet you are still attached. A master is unattached in the sense that attachment disintegrates much more quickly because he is much more centered in the moment than if he had never practiced. One could say that we live in nonattachment through attachment. Okay? Can you still consider me a Buddhist?"

Excerpted from *Fragments Zen: Mémoires de chair* by Philippe Rei Ryu Coupey, translated by Richard Collins and Isabel Collins

23. LOVE

Personal love can also become the Way, providing that it is precise. Love affairs have always been disturbing, even in Buddha's time. It is written in the *sutras*. Master Kodo Sawaki spoke about this too in his own *sangha*. Then Master Deshimaru spoke here in Europe, at Pernety, at the Val-d'Isère, at La Gendronnière about different love affairs which became disturbing. However, on this subject he said: "When you think about it you can see that love does not have such great importance in our lives, neither does sex." That is interesting because we always hear the opposite, and there are few people who can say that. Only those who have resolved this question of life and death, of love and sex can speak like that.

To make love, is it bad? Is it good? The Zen masters, the patriarchs, the ancestors, did they not make love? Fall in love? I imagine that even the great Zen masters, whether they were young or old, used to think about love, and even about sex, about being in the company of a woman, or a man. Some masters did, but without attachment. For example, we have the poems of sexual love by Master Ikkyu. Ikkyu was a Rinzai master, very virulent on the subject of institutionalized Zen. Ryokan and others also had love affairs. That did not change their understanding and their practice at all, as there was no attachment. How do we do it without attachment? It is up to each of us to go deep into this question. And in doing so we must not forget the question of compassion, of universal love.

I believe that we can desire or love without it becoming a terrible attachment, but an unconscious means of going further, and so bring true happiness to another. And what is that? Take away the person, the me, and do not take away the object, the other. In the end it is about how to live, how to understand the way things work, not just human beings, but the workings of the cosmos.

It is not a question of obliterating yourself, but rather of giving yourself to another. Giving, that is one of the six *Paramitas*,* or perfections. To give to others is to give to yourself.

24. DESIRES

We all have emotions. How many times in a day do we live through an emotional state? Deshimaru was also subject to emotions; he got angry. A true master is an emotional being, so it is not about abolishing them. That is what the *arhats** in Hinayana did: Snap! Emotions forbidden! Even thoughts were forbidden. But in Mahayana, we believe that the Buddha did not teach any prohibitions in any final or profound sense. So what do we do?

I think the problem is that we do not know how to connect with desire—with this energy, this warmth, which leads to desire. That is why most religions try to turn us away from it; they ban it, flee from it. However, it can also be useful to us.

There is the desire, for example, of wanting to be close to someone. But through regular practice, continuing on the Way, I think that we do not really get close to others, but to "it." Being close to "it" is to transform desires, to deepen them.

If we remain in the present, we do not fall into any traps: the trap of personal love, the trap of silence, the trap of the beauty of nature, the trap of marvelous and harmonious ceremonies...We are not captivated by anything whatever—the trees, the flowers, the sun, the rain, warmth, cold... Let us have pleasure, let us have joy, but we must not fall into those traps either. We must not be attached. That simply means not dwelling on anything. That is how you can really take pleasure in it. Not dwelling on anything means: not going from phenomenon to phenomenon, but from phenomenon to non-phenomenon and from non-phenomenon to phenomenon. That is the practice of Zen, in the dojo and everywhere else. Our practice—except during retreats—does not mean isolating yourself from anything. We live completely in society, we work in society and we practice zazen in society. No separation. What we do is completely extraordinary if you think about it just a little bit.

Ku and *Shiki*, essence and phenomena are not in duality with each other, that is, not opposed to one another. In zazen, awakening is not in duality with illusions. Awakening is neither cutting out the illusions nor going up into the mountains. In Mahayana Buddhism, we do not go up into the mountain, we *are* the mountain. We have to realize our ideal here and now. In any case the Four Bodhisattva Vows which we recite each morning come back to this: no separation. One of the four vows, "realizing all our desires,"[31] we realize them here and now. It is not that we cut them out, nor that we separate them from ourselves. There is not one side that is good and one side that is bad. We realize all our desires in the moment, in an instant. In an instant we go to the root, we do not rest on the surface of our desires. We would be wasting our time if we were tempted to try and resolve each desire one after the other, separating them from ourselves. There is no logic in this, it is not like mathematics; it is not "six times six equals thirty-six."[32]

Inmo. That is, suchness,* is also reality. But reality cannot be identified. So it is not necessary to abandon desires, but simply not to identify with them. That is "it."

---

31 The second vow: "However innumerable the passions, I vow to vanquish them all." To vanquish them is to realize them.

32 A similar expression to "six times six do *not* equal thirty-six" can be found in Daichi's poem no. 29 entitled "Buddha Nature": the four vows take place at a non-dualistic level.

25. ILLUSIONS

Many people notice that, in spite of the practice, they still have just as many illusions. In fact, something always remains with us. But this profound teaching has to be understood. "Profound" does not mean difficult; as Joshu* said, even a small girl of seven can understand it.[33]

For some practitioners, freeing themselves from the last residues of the subconscious is very difficult. I think this is because they never manage to undo the image they have of themselves. "This is me, that is you," or "I'm just like that, that's me." To be even more precise, you could say: "This is the artificial me..." Whatever it is, if you carry on in life without reflecting on yourself, the non-manifested karma will reproduce itself to infinity.

It is often said in the *sutras* that we wander around in life—we are cast adrift on the waves of illusions, and yet we always remain attached, until death: attached to the ego and material things. We love, hate, run away, follow. This is called "the ocean of life and death." But this is not really the case for everyone; it is not really the case for those who know, in the deepest sense, that there is no ego.

Illusions come from ego. We could say that the ego—our idea, our conception of "me"—only exists thanks to our illusions. In our profound and essential nature, what is the ego? It is *ku*: emptiness in every sense of the word. The ego exists, but it only exists as an illusion. That is why wanting to abandon the ego is a false concept. Abandoning an ego which is a fabrication of oneself by oneself is a total illusion, impossible to accomplish. It is still running after our own ego.

---

33 *Zen Commentary on the Numonkan* by Master Shibayama.

When the ego's sensitive layer is excited by phenomena, a reaction is triggered, a bit like the ocean—when the wind blows, waves appear. The term *bonno*, which is translated as "illusions," is interesting. It also means "the dust which comes to visit." *Bonnos* are visitors, therefore there is no need to be bothered by them. We can receive them like visitors. No need to slam the door in their faces; in any case they would then come in through the keyhole.

Sometimes we cut through them: "Cut!" Sometimes this word works, but sometimes it doesn't. So what should we do? Abandon them? Give in to them? I say it is better to observe them. By observing our own ignorance without judgement, we can bring them into a new dimension, like Nagarjuna* said in his commentary of the *Hannya Shingyo:* "The bodhisattva who is trying to understand his own nature must understand the nature of his own ignorance."

Bringing a new dimension does not mean making things disappear. The Christian saint is apparently transparent, perfect. But the Buddhist saint—that is us, who we really are, here and now, with our illusions and our karma. Our footprints do not disappear, something remains behind. That is us, here and now.

And so we can understand what the *Hannya Shingyo*, the *Heart Sutra,* is saying, that, for example, there is no ignorance nor the extinction of ignorance. Everything continues even after death. That is karma, the seeds of karma. The subconscious demonstrates this: we may not end fear or anxiety, but we must still observe, watch, search and find the venomous dragon or the soul of the fox.

In this way Buddha's light penetrates the waters of our illusions, penetrates through to our frozen bones, through to our most hidden illusions which are frozen in sleep. That is how we reabsorb the illusions through *ku,* which is also the dimension from whence they came. It could be that we are submerged in phenomena (stains, dust), but Buddha's light is there too. No need to get rid of it, to wipe away the dust; in any case we couldn't. Wisdom, enlightenment, is born out of dust, phenomena. So there is no need to flee or to run after anything.

Shiki simply becomes *ku* automatically and unconsciously. *Shiki soku ze ku*: form becomes non-form, ignorance becomes awakening. What is the difference between that and the waves of the ocean? The wave is the form the ocean takes; or you could say it is the cosmic *ki* of the ocean, its way of manifesting itself. You could also say that the wave is *shiki*, phenomena, and the ocean is *ku*, emptiness.

Because of this light of Buddha which shines into our most obscure illusions, we are able to awaken. This is Buddha's Zen teaching. A completely joyous teaching bringing good news.

26. KARMA

Karma is causes and their consequences. Everything is karma, you can't escape it.

Master Hyakujo* used to give talks after zazen. During these talks there was always an old man present amongst the other monks. He would listen and then leave. No-one knew him. One evening the old man did not leave; everyone had left the dojo except him. Master Hyakujo spotted him, went over and asked: "Who are you?"

The old man replied: "A long time ago, in the time of Kasyapa Buddha (that means before the birth of Buddha), I was the head of a temple situated on this mountain. A monk asked me this question: 'Is the enlightened man bound by the chains of karma?'

"I told him: 'I will never be bound by the links of the chain of karma.'

"Since that day I have never been reborn in human form but in the form of a fox. This has been so for 500 rebirths. You are a great master and you are on the mountain where this happened to me, so now I'm asking you, please give me the words that have the power to change this cycle, so that my body and mind can become a human being again."

Hyakujo listened very carefully; then the old man asked: "The man who has realized *satori*, is he bound by the chains of karma?"

Hyakujo came forward and replied in a loud voice: *"Fumai kuramasani!"* which means, do not cover up your footprints! Do not hide your footprints! In other words, you do not escape your karma...even a great master, even Buddha does not escape his karma.

You would think that this understanding of karma is shared by all Buddhists, but this is not the case. A long time ago I studied the works of Honen* and Shinran* (that is the Pure Land School), who teach what I understand to be exactly the opposite: the awakened human is freed from the chains of karma. That is not what Zen teaches.

Such a teaching creates a kind of deification, and it is a big mistake. A great master can cut the karma of another, but that does not mean that karma no longer exists. That means that one is freed from one's past karma, here and now, but karma continues: "Do not hide your footprints!"

That is why we have to go down to the depth of the mistake, to better shine a light on our illusions, our shadows: *Why do I do that? Why do I think that? Why am I angry with so and so? Why am I jealous of her or him?* If we do not do that, we are not being clear with ourselves or with others, which simply results in our going deeper into our complications. But each person is different, and each karma is different. Each one has their 500 lives, all different.

Little by little, as the years pass, for most people, life becomes more complicated. As children we only have our parents, but as we grow up friends appear, a partner, love, hate, jealousy. There is also work, competition. *Who will get the job? Me or someone else?* Then, when we get the job, we notice that we are always in competition with someone or other. At university, intellectuals are competing with each other. In affairs, it is the same thing. Even in unemployment and on welfare we are in competition. We get married, have children, get divorced, become old. That is karma becoming complicated. Then everyone around us starts to die, and one day it is our turn.

Certain ideas that we receive muddle things up even more. For example, the idea that our existence will get better. Everyone around us reinforces that idea and so reinforces our ego. Even in spirituality. We can become more and more complicated because of the spiritual way that we are practicing. And for that reason, in Zen, there are phrases like: "That trickster with the name of Shakyamuni appeared on this earth and led a lot of people astray." To take the metaphor further, instead of saying "this brilliant, sparkling morning star that awakened the Buddha," why not say, "this poisonous star"? You must really pay attention regarding the distortion (of the practice). For example: When you start practicing a discipline with your appearance—always speaking softly, always keeping a nice smile on your face,[34] adding water to what you eat to take away the taste, like the monks do in Thailand. They beg for their food, and if it is too good they add water and they do it publicly.[35] Or like the Japanese monks and nuns who have their clothes beautifully tailored in silk of fine quality. This is not the *dharma* converting us, but us converting the *dharma* to our own ego.

One can only affirm that karma is complicated at all stages and all levels. Little by little, as we grow up, we feel obliged to fit into the same mold as others. It is like that all over the planet, even in its most obscure corners. Everyone wears blue jeans; we all adopt the same mannerisms. In the jungle, in India or in the Amazon, everyone eats the same tins of food. In all European kiosks we find the same newspapers. More and more the same point of view dominates, the same gossip. Individuality is praised yet it is the great uniformity which dominates.

This is why it is so important to let the thoughts go in order not to get caught in the trap of all these things. But I would like to add that, only when we let go of our thoughts, can whatever remains in

---

34 "The external signs of a good Buddhist are a calm appearance, a serene manner, a gracious approach and a fresh colouring." *Memoirs of a Modern Gnostic* by Edward Conze, translator, writer and Buddhist erudite.

35 Some time ago I saw an article in a newspaper (*Bangkok Post*, 13/12/1991) showing a photo of a Thai monk eating his meal in a public park, surrounded by a number of admiring disciples. This article affirmed that, according to his 150,000 disciples living in Thailand and the United States, this very eminent monk was a living and enlightened bodhisattva.

The article went on to describe the way Phra Yantra fed himself: "In a slow and meditative way, he took the food from his bowl with his spoon... then he poured water into the food to diminish the flavour in order to show that he was not attached to the taste of the food...Each spoonful was chewed with serenity...And when it was finished he closed his eyes to continue his meditation... About 4 years later this same monk was defrocked and accused of "serious crimes" according to the newspaper *The Independent* of Bangkok, 12/11/1995.

our subconscious come out—those things which cannot come out in our everyday lives.

Without a regular meditation practice of looking inside ourselves, we cannot know the subconscious. Right from the beginning of our zazen practice we meet the subconscious, non-manifested karma—problems to do with our families, our parents, father, mother...An opening appears in the deepest consciousness thanks to the concentration on the posture, the breathing, not following the thoughts, and in this way non-manifested karma can emerge and be released.

With years of practice, the subconscious continues to manifest itself, but less and less. It also becomes more difficult to bring it out, since what is left is well hidden—repressed desires, non-materialistic desires, like succeeding in life, becoming someone...The subconscious is like a wound in the brain which cannot heal over, and the thoughts which come out of the subconscious are like pus coming out of this wound.[36] Of course, they must emerge, and through the continuous practice of zazen, soon there will be no more pus, and even no more healing over. Imagine no longer being influenced by your personal past. That would also mean not being influenced by the future. So, you do not create desires to become someone ... or, I don't know, what else. You do not create stupid karma. You are free.

However, it is different for everyone. There are people who come from a very troubled childhood—it was like that for me. They emerge perturbed, but they manage nevertheless to transcend it, more easily than those who had a peaceful childhood and yet still continue to carry all those heavy lessons and authoritarian demands. The latter usually come from quite balanced families, full of love; but the stupidity of education which is imposed upon children leaves them more traumatized than coming out of a nightmare.

You should not turn your back on your childhood; you must regain your true childhood. Even those who have lived without father

---

36 "Zen Pivots" by Master Sokei-An.

or mother have known powerful and important times, since a child is no different from an adult. Children who come from a troubled background are just as complete as any adult, troubled or not. They can also have some good memories and can feel alive and happy.

The importance of self-confession needs to be mentioned here, which means being honest with oneself. If you do not have a master, confess to yourself in front of a mirror and do *gassho*. For myself, I did not have too much difficulty in self-confessing in the master's room. He used to ask me questions about my particular way of earning my money, and about my overheated sexual behavior within the *sangha*, even in the *sesshins*. But then he knew how to make me talk, and I would tell him things that I had never told anyone else. In any case, it is more important to tell these things to yourself. Do not fool yourself. Do not lie to yourself but confess to yourself honestly all the time. It is important to express or try to express your mistakes. Everyone makes mistakes in little obscure corners. It is good to talk about them, not in a bar, lightly like that, but according to the teaching.

We must go to the root of our mistakes. We should not repeat mistake after mistake but go to the depths of the initial mistake. Otherwise, we will end up replacing the first fault with a second, and then a third, and so on. However, we must always pay attention; if we practice with a goal, even a very small goal, not only do we not cut our karma, but we perpetuate it, even during zazen.

There is no obvious way to correct our mistakes. For example, Buddha went from mistake to mistake. First of all, he stood on one leg for a year. Then he started to feed himself a single sesame seed and a single drop of water every day. Finally, when he found himself close to death, he sat under the bodhi tree and really looked at himself. He went directly to the depth of the fault.

We are not prisoners of our karma. Here and now we can be free of it. However, we are under its influence, like I said earlier, we are not outside karma when we are awakened. What I learned directly from Master Deshimaru was that even a great master has what we call "faults." It is true education when we see the master and we say: "I'm not going to behave like them, I hope." For that, you have to have faith in what the master represents and what he or she does.

Buddha died after having eaten pork, and that was in an era when it was forbidden to eat it. There have been debates on this subject and some people who fanatically support a vegetarian viewpoint say that he died because of his bad karma. Christ died another way; he was a martyr. This creates another karma, and Christian karma has a very pernicious aspect which is how martyrdom has spread throughout Christianity. There was not just Jesus, but also St. Peter, Joan of Arc, St. Sebastian and thousands of others. And Muslim karma is similar. Buddha himself never knew martyrdom—the idea never entered his head. It is a concept unknown in Buddhism—it cannot be found in Hinayana, nor in Mahayana nor with the Tibetans. If I am not mistaken, even the Vietnamese nuns and monks who burnt themselves alive during the Vietnam war have never been perceived as martyrs.

There have been enormous studies on karma, even before the birth of Buddha. After Buddha's death, Buddhism fell back on the ancient Hindu conception of karma. And in order to maintain that today, the ordinary people, the untouchables and women perhaps, say that their oppression is due to their bad karma, and that they must subject themselves to it in this life while hoping to progress in the next. This concept of karma is a way of imprisoning men, and women even more, and in the same way it favors those "well placed" in society through birth, like the Brahmans. References to karma in Tibetan Buddhism are of the same order, even in Tibetan Buddhism today,[37] but this is not karma.

37 Lati Rinpoche was asked if he believed that all those murdered during the course of the Holocaust deserved their deaths (that is to say that karma is understood like an expiatory principle). To which he replied: "The victims have gained their experience as a consequence of actions accomplished in previous lives..." (Extract from *Karma and Rebirth*, by Nagapriya, Windhorse Publications, 2004)

Buddha himself explains—and this is Zen teaching—that it is not the individual who continues or is reborn, but the action. That changes everything and opens up Buddhism and the idea of karma to something truly universal. The interpretation, the understanding of Buddha, his manner of explaining karma, seeks to free human beings not to imprison them.

Another idea that is spreading is that people with hunchbacks or with disabilities are born like that as a result of their bad karma. I think that, on the contrary, as Buddha said, the whole world's bad karma created by the acts of individuals, is not transmitted from individual to individual. And so, the people who have been suffering from birth should be the most respected, since they carry on their backs the bad karma of the whole world. Naturally I have never been able to take seriously the claim that there is a progression through successive rebirths, for example from a woman to a man, as is often said in those Asian countries which embrace the ideas of Hindu culture. Brahmanism is thus deeply ingrained, even in the Upanishads and the Vedas.*[38]

When he was 30 years old in the year 414, Jo Hoshi[39] was beheaded by the emperor. Jo Hoshi was a Chinese Buddhist monk, an extremely talented writer and a religious genius. He wrote a number of philosophical works. One day the emperor asked him to renounce his life as a monk and come to the palace to take up the post of imperial secretary. Jo Hoshi refused to obey, and the emperor had him beheaded.

An American Zen master said that Jo Hoshi was beheaded because he was paying for the bad karma of a previous life, that he knew for certain that he had committed some sort of capital crime.[40]

---

38 Of course, this is a grand simplification of the idea of karma. As the Buddha said himself, "Attempting to plan precisely the results of karma is something indeterminate upon which no conjecture can be made and which drives anyone who tries to do it to madness and torment." (Thanissaro, A IV.77)

39 Seng-Chao in Chinese (384-414). Highly talented Buddhist monk. The emperor had ordered Seng-Chao to return to lay life and to serve him as imperial secretary. Seng-Chao refused and he was executed. He was thirty years old.

40 *The Zen of Living and Dying* by Philip Kapleau, (Shambhala, 1998).

Of course, I disagree with this point of view. Holding an individual guilty for whatever occurred in a previous life, whether he is a monk or not, to me, shows a lack of deep perception. That is forgetting the interdependence among all human beings. Karma is not personal; if someone pays for their karma, they pay for the karma of us all, and for all of us, not as it is understood by this American master.

And so in Jo Hoshi's case, whether there is reparation or expiation, it is for the crimes of the whole world. That is why Jo Hoshi was a great monk and not an ancient murderer. To think that he gave his head simply for his own good is extremely immature.

Here is a poem that Jo Hoshi wrote just before his execution which really shows who he really was:

Originally the four elements have no master,
The five aggregates are essentially empty.
Now I face the sword with my head
Let us do it like hoeing the spring breeze.

So, there is no need to feel guilty about karma, saying to ourselves: "Oh I've got such a bad karma…" On the contrary. With a tough karma we can do something. His karma was tough too. You can see he struggled with it. No need to feel guilty, unless this guilt makes you really look at yourself, and so become free of it by understanding something much deeper about yourself. We are 100-percent responsible, but only in this life, in the present moment. The past is done, and the karma we have inherited from our families we cannot change. But we are responsible for what we are doing here and now. Here and now we can change everything.

I think that we are here precisely to resolve the problem of our karma, to change it, to raise it to another level. And that is the way we can help others, by not leaving dirty footprints, bad karma, for future generations to follow. Otherwise, they will inherit it directly and indirectly, you can be sure. To think that everything is over when we die is completely false. It continues. That is what we call *alaya** consciousness.

Our illusions continue too. After death everything that we have done is still there, like small seeds ready to germinate. That is what is reborn and comes back at the given moment. You might think: "It is not me, all this bad karma comes from someone else; it's not my problem." Mistake. Karma after death is no longer personal, yet you also cannot say that we are born here on this earth for nothing. We are here precisely for that. When we are born, it is because what we have done still exists. It is worsened or improved by the life we have led. We have come through cause and effect and for each one of us the cause brings us to the effect.

Once the earth disappears there will be other planets, other forms of human beings or karmic consciousnesses. In Buddhist teaching, there is neither beginning nor end. We have been following this tradition since Buddha, and all the teachings show us that there is no beginning or end. This planet will disappear, but not us. "Us" as individuals, yes, but life-consciousness will not disappear. Why should it disappear? The practice of the Way is a question of faith, of faith in life. That is to say, to trust in the human being—and so in oneself.

Let us look at and study our rebirths. We should not just look at what has happened in the last twenty years of our lives or when we were young. We have to look at all our lives—not our reincarnations in a petty sense of the word, like, "I was a prince in a past life."[41] Let us look at the last hundred years, the last two hundred years. Look at the pattern, how it has unfolded over time, and the beauty of that pattern.

---

41 Edward Conze, the celebrated expert Buddhist, translator and compiler of *sutras*, said of himself: "In a past life I was a noble Mongol lama from Tibet," and he even gave the approximate date. *Tricycle Magazine*, autumn 2004.

Christmas Humphreys, the important Buddhist writer, talks of the time he spent in ancient Egypt as a high graded officer in the entourage of Ramses II. *The Memoirs of a Modern Gnostic* by Edward Conze.

Reclining in Our Coffin, We Can Imagine Ourselves in a Bubble Bath

In the mid 1980s, I travelled with a friend to India where I took part, with some others, in a big Buddhist colloquium in Delhi.[42]

It was after this colloquium that a Sikh assassinated Prime Minister Indira Gandhi while we happened to be staying with some Sikhs. Thus, there was a lot of hatred and violence towards Sikhs.

My friend and I pretended to own the house while the entire Sikh family hid in the cellar. Because the Indians were pro-Russian Communists, when they knocked on our door we pretended to be Russian. They beat up a Sikh right there in front of our door. To compliment us on our great Russian nation, they warmly applauded us. Their hands were covered in blood.

Two lies to save our skin. Causes and effects. Everything we do comes back to us. We cannot escape, and each of our actions influences our future. But you could ask yourself the question: do I lie to benefit the Way or to advance my own ends? There is a difference between an elephant who turns its back on humans to conceal its precious defenses and a scientist who tampers with the genome to create cows without horns.[43]

If we lie to ourselves, we cannot see things as they are: reclining in a coffin, we can imagine ourselves in a bubble bath. It's about staying vigilant, even if things are going well. And if we are troubled by our mistakes and lies, it's good to talk about it: not in a bar, lightly, but seriously, as a kind of teaching evaluation.

There was a period when I had doubts about myself, about the quality of my education, and

---

42 The First Buddhist Council in Delhi, October 1984.

43 We are told by the industry magazine *Reussir--Bovine viande* (Succeed--Cow Meat): "In France, three breeds of milk cows are currently being looked into with the idea of creating animals genetically modified to lack horns. While the effort expended on this at the moment is marginal, the trend is on the rise" (23 September 2011).

I confessed all this to Sensei who helped me to see things more clearly. He believed it was important to confess to oneself; that is to be honest with yourself. Now that Master Deshimaru is no longer around and I am the one who is old, I continue this practice of confession by myself.

Understanding confession allows you to awaken to yourself, by yourself. If you do not have a master, you can confess in front of the mirror to yourself, by yourself. It is important to confess without going in search of someone to confess to.

The monk Dogen, who often appealed to the laws and teachings of nature, said in the Mujô-Seppô, one of the chapters of his principal work, the *Shôbôgenzo*:

> *All things, in our universe, have their own independence and their own dignity. The sun, the moon, the stars, the mountains, the rivers, the plants, the trees, the birds, the animals, the insects, the fish, all things, even those which seem inanimate, have their own independence and their own dignity or, in other words, possess fundamental life.*

Excerpted from *Fragments Zen: Mémoires de chair* by Philippe Rei Ryu Coupey, translated by Richard Collins and Isabel Collins

27. ORDINATION

Without a doubt, ordination is the best way of transforming our karma. In order to ask for ordination it is essential to have faith. If you have been practicing zazen for some years without ever having asked for ordination, you neither wear the *rakusu** nor the *kesa,* then, little by little, your zazen practice is reduced to a form of exercise or a hatha yoga posture.

Each morning we put our *rakusus* on our heads and chant the *Dai Sai Geda Puku** which is saying something like: "*Universal Garment (the kesa), now I have satori to help others! What a marvelous thing!*" Obviously, this goes beyond individual posture, beyond practicing for oneself or any personal and psychological well-being. Kodo Sawaki said: "You have to believe in the cosmos." But that is difficult, so the *kesa* or *rakusu* received at ordination is a very practical object of faith.

Asking for ordination is the actualization of our faith, our conviction. But there is no "when," no fixed date to receive it. In some *sanghas* you have to wait two or three years to become ordained bodhisattva, then another five years to become a monk. But in our way of practicing, it is about sensing through the body when the moment has arrived. I often recall that Eka,* the second patriarch in the Zen lineage, was never ordained.

Ordination is essential, but here we have Eka who never received it. That is all very profound and means that we should never get stuck on any category. It means we should never take up any position but remain not-two.

Even though the *kesa* or the *rakusu* is given at the moment of ordination, it is not the cloth which is transmitted. At the same time there is also the paper, the *ketsumyaku,* which is given to the ordained person, upon which is recorded the lineage of ancestors from Buddha through all the disciples, Indian and Chinese (Bodhidharma, Eka, Sosan, Eno, Fuyodokai, Nyojo*), then the Japanese (Dogen, Kodo

Sawaki, Deshimaru), down to us, in Europe. It is only on paper, and yet this line is written in red. This is the blood, it is written in blood. Of course we are talking symbolically; the blood symbolizes the body. That is to say, through the inside not through the outside.

The last conversation I had with Master Deshimaru, just before he went back to Japan where he died soon afterwards, was on this subject of ordination. I was with him at the airport. He wanted to go to the toilet but he didn't know where they were. I had just been there and I said to him: "Come with me I'll show you." On entering the toilets there was a *rakusu* hanging abandoned on one of the coat hooks! I turned to Deshimaru and said: "Who was the idiot who forgot his *rakusu?* And in the toilets too!"

He said: "Go and have a look." I looked more closely at the *rakusu.* It was mine!

Facing the wall in front of the urinals, Sensei turned to me and said: "You should never forget your *rakusu!*" And I replied: "Yes, but see, at least I removed it before taking a piss." Sensei smiled and insisted: "Ah, but do not forget your *rakusu.* Do not forget your ordination." Those were the last words he said to me. After that he left and then he died.

One day I had dinner with the Japanese master Nishiyama roshi and two or three of Deshimaru's disciples. This Japanese master claimed to have been a disciple of Kodo Sawaki. One of Master Deshimaru's old disciples, perhaps trying to flatter this master, said that Kodo Sawaki had been the greatest master of the twentieth century. I became angry: "How could you say such stupid things? You never knew Kodo Sawaki, everything you know about him came from Deshimaru! You're afraid of the true dragon, and you're running after paper dragons! You only know Kodo Sawaki on paper. The greatest master is your own master! But you don't even know that!"[44]

---

44 Shortly after Deshimaru died, this disciple left his teaching to follow Nishiyama before going on to follow Narita, another master in the Kodo Sawaki lineage.

Do not forget your ordination, and do not forget from whom you received it. My co-disciple Étienne Zeisler* told me that someone came up to him one day and said: "I'm sure I know you from somewhere," to which he replied: "Yes, I ordained you." You should try not to forget these intimate moments you have lived through with your master, and especially ordination. Ordination is always intimate, and it is forever.

Once ordained, a person can no longer be negligent of his or her life. Master Deshimaru said to me one day: "Now that you are my disciple and a disciple of Buddha you should not risk your life for silly things." These words may seem anodyne, but they really struck me at the time because I thought that a true human being always risked their skin. I was also influenced by the lives of the samurais. It has been written that a true samurai dies young. But a samurai, I suddenly realized deeply, is not a monk.

Also, when we take ordination, it is inevitable that we take other people with us, and obviously we should not lead them off in the wrong direction. One of my disciples was a canoeing guide. For his ordination I gave him the name "Calm River, Exact Mind" and yet he died with two other people whom he was accompanying in the turbulent Verdon Gorges, a river canyon in southeastern France. He did not use his exact mind.

It is better to listen, to understand the name you receive at ordination, the monk's or nun's name. In any case it is not me who gives the names, you should understand that too. I am also a guide, but my job is to bring people to eternal life not to a sudden death. Having said that, this disciple[45] was a man with a big heart, always ready to give, and it seems that when the wave came upon them in the canyon, he acted like a hero; he tried to save the lives of the two other people with him, but in vain, and all three were drowned. Of this I have no doubt; he was prepared to give his life for others.

---

45 Arno Richards

28. THE BODHISATTVA

In our lineage most people first ask for the ordination of bodhisattva, followed by that of a monk. Generally, the person who asks for this ordination takes the precepts and wears the *kesa*, or simply the *rakusu*: that means that they have entered into Buddha's teaching like a son or daughter of Buddha.

To take care of oneself is to take care of all human beings. According to the Mahayana doctrine this is the correct point of view. Whereas in Hinayana it would be: to take care of yourself is to actualize you own enlightenment. And after you have attained it you become an *arhat*,* not a bodhisattva. Now if you take care of yourself for the sake of the entire earth you become a bodhisattva. I think this is one way to explain the difference between Mahayana and Hinayana. Having said that, we of the Mahayana, as I have said before, all come from the Hinayana. We all begin with the small path. Buddha also started like that, then he became bodhisattva.

29. BECOMING A NUN OR MONK

Asking for ordination is for the well-being of the sangha, the community. It must be deeply understood that receiving the monk's ordination is not a stage that comes after the bodhisattva ordination. The bodhisattva ordination is complete in itself like the face of the moon. The same goes for the monk's ordination. Being ordained a monk generally comes from a desire to continue following the teaching of the person who gives the ordination.

Becoming a monk, becoming a master, does not mean automatically that you go off to live in a monastery or a temple; that you leave the conjugal home. It's true that in Zen the great monks of the past lived alone, but this is not really the case today. Suzuki Roshi* lived with his wife, Maezumi lived with a woman, however Master Deshimaru lived alone. He used to say: "It is not obligatory to live alone, but it is easier for practicing the Way."

What are the true merits of being ordained a monk? Bodhidharma would have replied: "No merit at all." But if you become a monk or nun you live for other things besides yourself. You shave your head, although that is not obligatory; you change your clothes, you no longer wear everyday clothes in the dojo, you wear the habit of a monk or nun. That is to say, you wear almost the same clothes as were worn two or three thousand years ago—that is important, since we are not any different from the people who lived in Buddha's time. At the same time, we are different from people today who follow fashions and change their clothes every year.

The *kesa* or the *rakusu* symbolize the Buddha mind, the transmission of the Buddha mind through Mahakashyapa to our own master and then to us. On becoming a monk, and that is the same for each person who practices, you live for something higher than your small self. And that way you completely change the world.

The monk can perhaps be compared to a diamond which absorbs and reflects all colors, but of itself has no color. That does not mean that he or she has no character or personality, but exactly the opposite. By way of being in contact with original nature, they can take on all the colors of the rainbow. And so, while they are similar or identical to others, they are also different. They are not hindered by anything, especially not by the mind, not by opinions and prejudices. They are *unsui*.*[46] That is the image of clouds and flowing water; the Zen monk flows like the water in a river, always new, always fresh. The monk or nun passes by like a cloud without being fixed or attached to anything.

Becoming a monk or nun is also about giving: there is no need to spend money like water, making donations to various causes. If a monk or nun has money, they can give it to others who practice, and that's because the Dharma helps more than anything else; it helps in the invisible. Isn't that an extraordinary merit? Changing the world and leading it away from sinfulness... Sinfulness?—What is that? Ignorance that is mind in error. And, "Sin is always a regression," wrote Meister Eckhart, "from oneness to multiplicity."[47]

The monk or nun tries to go beyond their karma, you could say their destiny, but this cannot be explained logically. It is not a question of renouncing material things like house or family. You do not need to become a monk or nun for that. Freedom in our lives, whether we are monks, nuns, or not, is not really logical. But if you want to help others, transmit the Buddha's teaching and continue this transmission that you have received, then becoming a monk or nun is the most efficient way to do it, since simply wearing the *kesa* changes one's state of mind. That is where beginning and end change meaning.

Our practice is eternal kindness. This is a great merit, for us, for our ancestors, and for all who came before us in our family because they have here and now produced a true monk or a true nun who can change the karma of their father and mother, who change the karma of the whole world.

---

46 *Un*: cloud. *Sui*: water

47 See: *The Eastern Buddhist*, August 1995

30. MASTER AND DISCIPLE

It is very difficult when one is not in contact with a master to practice intensely; to do *sesshins*, to spend one or two months in a summer camp. If you are not linked to a master, that is to say, linked by faith to what the master has faith in, then what is going to make you practice? You have to have courage to follow a master, and so be pulled along by the nose-ring, to use one of Master Dogen's expressions.[48] The person who represents Kodo Sawaki, or Bodhidharma, or Buddha, to another is the one who can pull this nose ring.

It is essential to practice intensely. If you do not do summer camp, for example, then your practice remains superficial; you can only stagnate. Stagnating is worse than going backwards. When you go backwards you discover the joy of going forwards. But if you fall onto a bed and pull the blankets over your head, you could remain like that, not only for the rest of your life, but for a whole series of lives.

We disciples of Master Deshimaru used to spend two months at every summer camp. Sometimes someone had to leave a bit early for fear of losing their wife or husband or their work, but we would always work things out.

In every contact there is a transmission, and this transmission is not just one-way. Most of the masters who have disciples practice a lot of zazen. I go to zazen seven times a week, and that is because the people around me are pulling me by my nose-ring.

A true master is always in the process of learning, of practicing the Way as best they can. There is no difference between master and disciple. The master, like the disciple, the patriarchs like the demons, are all human beings born of a father and a mother; born out of

---

48 The second poem of Dogen's Eheikoroku begins: "We must pull ourselves along by our own nose-ring..." Mon Corps de Lune, by Philippe Coupey. Ed. (Adverbum 2008.)

karma. It is also useless to judge the master. Is he or she awakened? Have they received the true transmission from their master? For me these questions are a mistake. It is something that one should know unconsciously. When someone meets a true master and then asks, "are they awakened or not?" that just indicates that this person asking the question is not awakened at all. When you meet a true master you can say "That is a master." But how do you know? By their external charisma? By their actions? Buddha turned the flower naturally in his fingers and Mahakashyapa reacted unconsciously. The actions of Buddha and Mahakashyapa do not have any conscious reasoning, any more than do the actions of a master and disciple.

At the beginning of the Sixties, the famous poet Allen Ginsberg* went to India to look for a guru. From what he said, his intention was to disappear in India for several years in search of wisdom. Certainly all of us have some rather stunted ideas about the true spiritual way when we begin; we think it is something external that we can take from someone wiser than ourselves. But Ginsberg, along with his friends, said in the end that he did not find anything, neither in India nor in Japan where he went afterwards. He said that he learned nothing because he did not have any true instruction. And why did he not have any true instruction? Because he did not know how to ask for it. He met many masters, many gurus, *swamis*, but he never asked a single question about the practice, about the actual way of practicing. He said himself that he was a bit too stupid to know what it was all about.[49]

Today, perhaps things are simpler in our practice—it is open to everyone. We have people coming from all walks of life, both social

---

[49] "I went to India principally to look for a master. I thought I would disappear in India for a few years..." Ginsberg wrote, already famous at the time. "... and I would find some wisdom." Then he went to Japan with some friends and took part in a *sesshin* at Daitoku-ji. "But," he said "I learned nothing apart from the correct instructions. The problem was that I didn't know what to ask. I went in search of a master and I saw several swamis, but I didn't really know how to ask. In fact I was too dumb." *Shambhala Sun*, July 1994.

and economic. We have the middle class, the workers, the marginals, the discontented, the troublemakers, crazy people.

Masters in ancient times used to select their disciples. Crazy people were turned away and so were the troublemakers. Today, for better or worse, people can come no questions asked. One can even proclaim oneself a disciple up to the moment when a serious and unpleasant exchange with the master happens, and then storm out slamming the door, without ever thinking that a teaching has just been given.

Also, some people are too fragile, in the sense that they are too easily hurt. Sometimes the master has to be hard, but sometimes can make a mistake and be too hard with someone. Once, Deshimaru refused to let me enter the dojo; I had to work on the roof of the new building at La Gendronnière; I worked during all the zazens of one entire summer camp. He said that I did not understand anything. But that was a good thing because, in the end, I knew that I would never leave this practice with him for anything in the world. He knew that too and that is very important. A master cannot be so severe with a disciple unless the master has complete trust in them. However, even though the master may have complete trust in a person's mind, they can still go too far and break that person.

It is quite delicate. I think that a master on the Way does make mistakes. Kodo Sawaki used to say that unfortunately a master breaks three people by perhaps being too brutal, by getting angry before understanding and correcting their errors. It's a tragedy but that is how it is. A master can get too angry or even be dishonest, mean or greedy. And then a disciple may leave and never come back.

It is not easy for a disciple to keep the right distance from the master. This relationship is like a fire—stand too far and you freeze, come too near and you burn. You should not want to be too close; you cannot play if you are too close. A certain distance is always necessary. The master-disciple relationship is a relationship of friends but not in the ordinary sense of the word.

Each person must define the word "master" for themselves. But for disciples, the master is the one who points them to the path, the Way; not just through the master's teaching in the dojo and behavior outside, but also because the master is beyond him- or herself and beyond the disciple. The master is the one who can transmit their own master's teaching, and the disciple is the one who is receptive to that teaching and that practice.

Master and disciple are united in the depths of the practice with the mind of *I shin den shin*,* heart to heart, my mind to your mind. Master and disciple, disciple and master, it is a relationship for the mutual purpose of the *dharma*. And the work of each practitioner is to transmit the *dharma* automatically, unconsciously and naturally. To transmit that which has been transmitted across the centuries and which will be transmitted for centuries to come; and without the intervention of free will.

My Lunar Body

The man facing me was playing with a heavy ashtray. He fixed his gaze on me, on the ashtray, then again on me.

We were seated in one of the bars in the Berlin airport. The Swiss disciples who accompanied me, two big, strong men, didn't quite grasp the situation and were happily occupied drinking beer and watching people in the airport. We were returning from a *sesshin* in northern Germany, and it was one of those rare moments of relaxation before we had to catch the flight back to Paris. I was trying to think of a way to stop this guy who seemed bent on cracking my skull open with that ashtray.

In fact, I knew him. It was Gunther, a close disciple I had recently forbidden to attend *sesshin*. His mental state had been greatly deteriorating for quite some time. He had developed schizophrenia which made him more and more aggressive. Zazen might have aggravated the illness. It locked him in with his thoughts. He became completely imprisoned by them. The psychiatrists in Berlin had deemed him incurable.

What could I do but forbid him to come?

It all started when he injected cement into the locks at the dojo in Berlin.

A little later, he attacked the responsible of the dojo with a stick in the middle of zazen before throwing him a piece of leopard-print clothing while shouting, "Take that, you dirty faggot! Here's a monk's robe for you!"

I had ordained Gunther and given him the monastic name "Peace of the Sangha." Clearly, he wasn't exactly living up to his name.

In the end, Gunther did not attack me at the airport. On the contrary, he was happy to see me. He even started a conversation, and from then on it became our ritual: after each *sesshin* in Germany we met up in the airport. We saw each other once a year and caught up. Not a complete separation but rather a healthy distance.

After our discussion Gunther stuck with us until baggage claim and, while saying goodbye, threw himself down in front of me yelling, "Thank you, great master—Allahu Akbar!"

This was just a few weeks after the attack of the Twin Towers on 9/11.

Of course, the German police immediately rushed towards us and Gunther had some explaining to do.[50]

On returning to Paris a few hours later, I entered my studio and greeted Hotei, the big-bellied monk who carries a hemp sack and bursts into laughter, the index finger of his right hand pointing upward. Hotei is a wooden statue in my library and what he points at is the moon.

The mortal moon hath her eclipse endured.—Shakespeare, Sonnet 107

Often in Zen one refers to the moon as a symbol of the mind, of *hishiryo* consciousness, thought beyond thought, beyond the mental state. It is the moonlight, the beautiful moon.

Not only in Zen, but in the arts in general, the moon has always inspired poets and musicians. Shakespeare talks about it in his sonnets; Beethoven, in his "Moonlight Sonata."

The moon evokes not just wisdom and clarity of mind. It also arouses sadness, melancholy, the passage of time, the trials of life, tears that fill up an entire night, and a mournful wind.

Here is another verse from an English poet:

With how sad steps, O Moon, thou climb'st the skies!—Sir Philip Sidney (1554-1586)

As Master Daichi Sokei (1290-1366) says in a poem dedicated to Master Keizan:

The melancholy sound of the koto spreads its breath over the entire Earth.

The *koto* is a stringed instrument, so here it's not the sadness of the moon, but the sadness of the wind.

The moon journeys upward into the sky and the higher it climbs, the more we are flooded with sadness.

Sadness is not a bad thing. We all live moments of great sadness. For example, when you see corpses not only in the morgue but on their deathbed. You find a body

50 Gunther practiced martial arts and was very physically strong. Yet he died in hospital from "falling downstairs."

inert, cold, a body belonging to a member of your own family, your mother, your father, your brother, your sister, your fiancée. When you are witness to that and you are still young, it makes you think. It brings you back to your own death. To reflect like that, without finding an answer, is to return to ground zero.

At this moment, the moon is neither
melancholy nor sad.
The moon is your own profound
nature.

Excerpted from *Fragments Zen: Mémoires de chair* by Philippe Rei Ryu Coupey, translated by Richard Collins and Isabel Collins

31. FROM MY SOUL TO YOUR SOUL

One day Master Deshimaru said that if a master and disciple dream about each other in the same moment then that is completely *i shin den shin*, from my soul to your soul.

These kind of "coincidences" happen all the time to those who do not obstruct them. It is no good, looking for the soul-to-soul connection or occurrence between master and disciple, since, if you grant it any particular value then you create an obstruction. One can easily create all sorts of ideas, undercurrents and mysteries and then lose the Way.

A little later, after he had spoken about this, I had a dream that Master Deshimaru was calling to his secretary Anne-Marie because he wanted an orange juice. It was quite late at night and she did not come because she was asleep. In the same moment I said to myself in my dream: "Ah I cannot bring him an orange juice because it is too far to go to get to his place." In short, it was quite an important dream. The next morning in his *kusen*, Deshimaru told us exactly the same thing: that he had been calling to his secretary for her to bring him an orange juice and she had not heard him. So I went to see Deshimaru after zazen to tell him: "Do you know what, I dreamt exactly the same, Sensei, I swear it's true!" He congratulated me: "Ah! Good! *I shin den shin*" I remember it because it was quite extraordinary, but nothing more than that.

32. STUDY

Knowing all the *sutras*, all the Buddhist texts, without practicing zazen is useless. It is just knowing things. I sometimes tell people they must study, but only people who practice zazen. If you do not *practice* zazen and yet you *study* Zen Buddhism, that is not Buddha's teaching. Perhaps studying Buddhism more and more and writing books on the subject will help you to get a well-paid job in a university. However, if you practice the Way assiduously, that probably won't get you a good job in Buddhism. Not at all.

Today in the United States, erudite and religious scholars find themselves attributed with more grants for Zen and for studies of Master Dogen's *Shobogenzo* than for any other subject.[51] They study Dogen, who ironically said: "Don't spend your time studying, just practice zazen." The professors and erudites cannot really understand zazen. Also, it is difficult to understand something so simple, especially for a mind that always functions through the fundamentally non-spiritual non-religious frontal brain. And what's more, how can you understand something like Zen meditation if you don't practice it correctly and profoundly yourselves?

Tokusan* died in 865. He was a great Buddhist scholar, and particularly of the *Diamond Sutra*.* Tokusan had two great shocks in his life. One was his meeting with an old woman who sold rice cakes, the other a little later with the Zen master Ryutan.* He became his disciple. Tokusan the great erudite burnt all his books after this second shock and went on to follow Ryutan, completely and exactly, until he himself became a great Zen master of the lineage.

Sometime before his meeting with Ryutan and the old woman, Tokusan had said: "I have mastered the *Diamond Sutra*. I am the supreme master of this *sutra*, of both its understanding and

51 Professor Bielefeld. *Sotoshu Journal*, 1992

interpretation." In fact, he had written twelve volumes of commentaries on this *sutra*; the depth of his discourses was incomparable. He was, like I said, the greatest erudite of his time and, though he did not do zazen at all, and did not have a master, he still claimed to be the supreme authority on the *sutras* of the practice.

His contemporary, Ryutan, only practiced zazen and was much less known than Tokusan. The latter said to himself: "I am going to meet this so-called great master and I am going to test him." So Tokusan went off to meet Ryutan armed with a number of volumes of the *Diamond Sutra*. On the way he met an old woman selling rice cakes. Tokusan wanted one, but she said to him; "Tell me worthy professor, what have you got in that huge bag?" The professor replied: "Have you not heard of me, the master of masters of the *Diamond Sutra*?"

"No, not really, but could I ask you a question? If you can answer me you will have a cake, otherwise you won't get one. I have heard this *sutra* recited a long time ago and it is said therein: '*The mind cannot be grasped neither in the past, nor in the present, nor in the future.*' So, Master, I ask of you: if you buy a rice cake, with what mind will you eat it?"

Tokusan was dumbfounded, he did not know what to say. A Zen master would not have had trouble with this question, but for a professor it was not obvious, even for a great *sutra* specialist. Seeing his face, the old woman concluded: "Well, great professor, you won't get any rice cakes to eat today!"

There is a great difference between acquired knowledge and the living experience. And if zazen is not the ultimate living experience, then I don't know what is. In any case, Tokusan continued on his way with an empty stomach, his spirit shattered, when at last he met Ryutan.

Men, women, our civilization, our culture certainly, all need great written works, but what is more important? Great works or great people? You might conclude that the world needs great women or great men, but not great works. According to Master Rinzai* who would often speak about "the man with no qualities," following the Way does not require special qualities. Courage is not a quality. Master Kodo Sawaki used to say that in order to become conscious of reality, and get rid of the blindfold—and that is exactly what zazen does—you need courage and *sang froid.* That is not quite the same for a specialist writer, even though writers do like to be spoken of as courageous. Their courage remains purely intellectual and has nothing to do with the courage of he or she who plunges body and mind into the Way.

In modern civilization, form has become our only way of relating to the world, and generally words are only useful for creating an image of a form. It is not an act of going beyond. It is not an act of the unknown, for example, in the sense of *sanpai,* as it was for primitive humans. It was not the *image* of *sanpai* in this one's head; no, the primitive simply did *sanpai,* the *act* of *sanpai.* There was the human, and there was the unknown, the human linking to the universal; the human was only the universal. Today the human is the individual who must succeed, who must develop a strong sense of self.

Words can heal, but that depends on how you read them. If you read Zen texts and *kusens* quickly in order to get to the end, that will not be effective at all. It also depends on what you read. If you read essential Zen texts like the *Shin Jin Mei,** the *Sandokai,** the *Hokyo Zan Mai,** the *Gion Shogi* by Fuyo Dokai* or certain chapters of the *Shobogenzo* like the *Zazenshin*, unconsciously you should spend a lot of time, even on each word. If you read general Buddhist texts, you will probably only spend a few seconds on each word. It depends how you read them. Some masters even put the Mahayana and Hinayana *sutras* into this category. They say, "If you do not understand these commentaries on the original Zen texts and only read other Mahayana *sutras*, you do not understand true Zen."

I think you could say that the Zen texts I have just quoted came *before* the *sutras*. It is true that the *sutras* were only composed a few hundred years after Buddha's death, and the Zen texts more or less a thousand years afterwards, but the *sutras* came after Buddha's awakening whereas the texts *are* awakening itself. That is understanding through the gut, here and now, like the Buddha under the bodhi tree; same space-time, same awakening.

When Master Deshimaru was alive, I remember that, before going to the dojo in rue Pernety, if I knew what he was going to talk about, I would study that subject early in the morning in order to understand better what he spoke about. On my way to the dojo I would wonder what he was going to say today about *satori*, how was he going to express it... It was never: what will come out of his mouth? But rather: what will come out of *ku*? That was a very strong impression. After zazen, we would go to the Café du Metro,[52] and our words at the counter really did return to *ku*.

---

52 As well as the Café l'Aurore across the street—"chez Tonton" as we called it.

33. THE TEACHING

You may not always follow the teaching given by the master—the teaching can come from someone else. And in the end, who is your master? It is the clouds, the sky, the moon...

You could say that the master does not teach anything, he or she only actualizes it. That is to say that the teaching arises out of *ku* in all its power. Our teaching begins with Buddha turning the flower before Mahakashyapa, and has nothing to do with the written word. Most Zen stories are not *written* anyway: Hotei's* finger pointing to the moon,[53] Gutei's thumb.

You must not depend on words. It is not Zen prose that will help us . . . beautiful writing, a well-turned phrase. Today, everything is about form. "Ah it is well-written, that is beautiful. What a lovely sentence." Once I read in a *sutra* a passage about the "Apocalypse" (where the question of *Kali Yuga** arose—the *era* when the essence of Buddhist teachings gets lost). This passage said that a sign that the teaching is degenerating is when one starts to write beautiful phrases and transform everything in this way, emptying it of its content.[54]

So, what is the teaching? It is *I shin den shin*, heart/mind to heart/mind.

You could say it is about an education which goes beyond the education of the frontal brain. The education that we have all received in our childhood ignores the deep brain. In the end, it ignores the entire

---

53 Suggesting that you should not confuse the moon with the finger that points to it. Look at the moon, not the finger.

54 "On the subject of Tathagata's sermons... The day will come when they are no longer considered as something to be studied and understood; on the contrary, they will become discourses made by poets in a poetic style, with embellishments and exaggerated ornaments, spoken by laymen who have been welcomed as scholars, and at that time the discourses of the Buddha will disappear."

character of the students, the thing which keeps them alive and makes them grow. A contact with something great, pure, holy and universal, present in each student—whatever their grade and their age; this thing which has no color, sound or taste, this is what a master unveils when they succeed in having a true relationship with the disciple.

There are three methods of education in Zen: *haju*, *hoko* and *setoku*. *Haju* means to capture. *Hoko* is to release. And *setoku* is to cut the karma by the teaching, *kusen*. In Zen education, you should always rotate the three methods, especially the first two: capture, grasp and release, liberate. If the master knows how to capture, at the same time they must know how to let go. It's a bit like flying a kite: very often you have to pull, very often you have to let go. I know this method well, but through experience, and I have learnt that there are all sorts of variations on this, holding on, letting go.

Often you catch the disciple by the tail—you catch them in their illusions. But sometimes that is of no great use since, while you hold them by the tail, nothing changes, you just hold the tail… and nothing... so you then go on to the *hoko* method, the second, the opposite method, to free, to release the person. That is the point when the master shrugs shoulders and says: "Do what you like..."

But, in some cases, the third method is essential: *setoku*, the teaching. The teaching of one's own master, which is the seed, a seed of karma in the *alaya* consciousness of the disciple. *Alaya* is the fundamental consciousness of all existence. Sometimes this education or transmission can be gentle; the relationship between Master Dogen and his disciple Ejo was gentle, although with others it was not at all. Sometimes Master Dogen banned certain disciples from entering the dojo. With Master Deshimaru it was the *kyosaku* and the *rensaku*.* One of his close disciples, one of his pillars, received it very severely one day in the summer camp at Val-d'Isère. This disciple never came back. Transmitting the teaching can be a brutal affair. Personally, I never received the *rensaku* from Sensei, but I was banned from entering the dojo, simply because one day I told him I was fed up with working for him. There was never a moment to spare, I had no personal life anymore. I had a wife, a child, I couldn't even see them. I lost them...but so what, I found them again another time, at a deeper, better level.

In order to follow the master I had to live alone. And when I said to him: "I am not writing any more books for you!" he replied, "In that case, you are banned from the dojo!" But of course, he let me in again a few weeks later.[55]

So, to come back to the third method, *setoku*. Even if we say in Zen there is one transmission which does not rely on words, we have to know how to make use of words and, whenever we speak, we must speak distinctly whether we are a master or just an ordinary practitioner. We must not mince our words, unreliable as they be. The dignity of the spoken word is important, it can represent the body and the mind. The Master always used to say that Zen was beyond words, but he also used to say that Zen words are like lights glittering in the darkness, coming out of *ku* and going back again. He used to talk like that.

That is why *kusen*s are very important. Perhaps they are less so if you live all day in a temple or a monastery where talks and *teishos* (conferences) are given regularly, and *mondo*s, or *dokusan** are held publicly and privately, where there is time allocated for the study of texts and *sutras*, and time allocated to learn them by heart.

Master Deshimaru developed the *kusen* himself[56] (*Ku* means teaching, *sen* means the mouth, *kusen*: oral teaching given during zazen) intended for people living in society and who do not have much occasion to listen to the teachings.

55 He actually even asked me to return to the dojo before my time was up.

56 He said of this: "Why do I speak during zazen? This practice of *kusen* comes from my master who himself received it from his master." (*I shin den shin*, 25th June 1976.)

But these three methods of education have nothing to do with accumulating anything, of remembering anything. It is not information. If I give a talk, I address it directly to the frontal brain—it is information. And remembering with the frontal brain is only another human mechanism which just adds to the baggage of knowledge. This does not hold a lot of weight, not in the long run anyhow. The knowledge I am talking about can be compared to forging a sword: You put it in the fire time and time again to sharpen it until it cuts. This is no longer information, but repetition. It is looking from one side to the other, looking at it from high to low, seeing it from all four directions, unconsciously and naturally.

I heard a number of *kusen* spoken by the Master during the 70's, and I do not remember a thing. However, for some years now I have been trying to give the same teachings, not through my memory, but through the body. The body is immortal, but not the human body: *the* Body. When Buddha remembered his past lives, it was not through the head, but through the body, the *Dharmakaya*. I have already spoken about this.

In terms of *kusen*, some Buddhist specialists say that we should not give commentaries on Daichi or Dogen without knowing the *kanji** precisely, the original ideograms. Naturally I don't agree with that at all. Because if this were true, then I couldn't even open my mouth once. I must say that I use Master Deshimaru as the base of my reference. He did not look for the exact meaning of the *kanji*; he was transmitting a teaching, and as a teacher of the dharma myself, I see it this way too.

One day I was working on a translation with him that was not at all clear, so I said: "But Sensei, what does all that mean? Give me a little time and I will make it a bit clearer." He shook his head: "Not necessary, not necessary!"

"But Sensei, it's for publication!"

"So?" he smiled, and then said in a different tone of voice, "If it's too clear people will go away."

"Oh yes, I see," I replied, shaking my head in agreement.

Yes, because unfortunately, at that moment, people think they have understood something, if not everything. We have seen it so often over the years: "I understand now, no need to continue any longer." But I think that what is missing for these people who stop practicing is that they have not understood that it is a practice without understanding, without goal, without end. That, they could not grasp. They have certainly understood the posture, but have they understood *muso*, the non-posture? Is that able to be understood? Can the wind be understood? And the full moon?

This is why Zen texts and poems use a lot of symbols to pass on the teaching. It is effective to think in terms of symbols, since symbols are too immaterial for us to become attached to them. They can never be fixed into dogmas and concepts; indeed, symbols are alive, they can become greater than themselves, and they do not belong to any culture, religion or society in particular. They are international, universal, and so mistakes cannot be made when we think symbolically.

The situation, the circumstances, also play an extremely important part in Zen teaching. The first time I heard the voice of Master Deshimaru—it was in the Paris dojo, at rue Pernety. I had been practicing for about two weeks every day, but Sensei wasn't there. He was directing a *sesshin* somewhere else, a long *sesshin*. One day two weeks later I heard his voice behind me. At first I did not even realize it was a human voice, it was like the noise of rocks crashing together in a torrent. Afterwards I understood that it was a person, that it was the Master who was speaking. At first, I thought that he was speaking Japanese, and then, little by little, I realized that he was speaking English, a funny kind of English. The situation was perfect. It was very early in the morning. Silence everywhere. Then suddenly the rocks crashing, then words in English. He stood up and then the next words he spoke were directly behind me. When words are powerful like that, when something is being transmitted, you get the impression that it is only for yourself. And it *is* only for yourself, there *is* only one. And at that moment he said: "In Zen, there is nothing to obtain!" I had a really strong reaction to that.

It is not really the content of the words. The content, the sense of the words can be found anywhere—in books, dictionaries, in the *sutras*. You can hear them in cafés, in the street. But it is also the place, and the unconscious expectation. It is the presence of other people, the silence, the stillness, the crashing of the rocks, a voice, a language, a turn of phrase, and then thirty years later, maturity. I think it is like that for everyone if you are available.

34. SILENCE

One day a practitioner in the Paris dojo was being interviewed for a television program. He was asked: "What is the most important teaching that your master has given you in the Paris dojo?" He replied: "Finding silence." That sounds really good, but is it true?

Master Deshimaru never stopped giving *kusen*s, oral teachings in the dojos. But where did these sounds, these words come from? They came from before thought, before personal thought, from non-duality. And because of this, his dojo was completely silent. Completely *ku*.

What is silence? We think it is a question of sound, of noise, or, in this case of no sound, no noise. We think that silence is when we no longer hear the cars passing, people speaking, birds singing, but that is not silence at all. Silence is not *something*, it is not something to look for. Silence is not something that happens when the door is closed. Silence is not the lack of something. And likewise, zazen is not sitting in silence. It is not sitting in stillness either, but quite the opposite. It is sitting in the sounds, in the movement, in total movement. Everything is there, all the sounds of the world. Silence is the birds singing, the crickets chirping, the frogs croaking. Silence is the wind in the trees.

Who are we before our birth, before the birth of our parents? That is silence. That is the silence that is always present. That is existence; existence without noumenon. Silence is our original nature and our breathing, it is the thought that becomes non-thought and the non-thought that becomes thought. That is the cosmos, the silence of the cosmos, the coming and going of thoughts. Silence is what is.

We should not be bothered by this question of silence or non-silence. As Master Hyakujo said: "Running away from noise and looking for silence is like throwing away the flour and looking for the bread."

35. *KOANS*

When thinking about Zen teaching one often thinks about *koan*s. In intellectual circles today, *koan*s are seen as "enigma," but that too is a mistake. A *koan,* or rather the solution to a *koan*, is not an enigma, simply because the solution is not a thought, a mental fabrication.

Most of the problems of communication with other people, even people with whom we are most intimate, come from the attachments we create through language. The purpose of the *koan* is to free us from these shackles in our heads, to free us from the limited preconceptions which come from a single point of view, the human point of view.

As an example, here is a famous *mondo* between Master Joshu and a monk, during the ninth century, CE. One day a monk asked Joshu,

At the top of the Bastille Column

"The solution of a koan is not a thought."

"Does a dog have Buddha nature?" And Joshu replied "*Mu!*"* "*Mu*" at least in this case means "has not" or "none." But a "has not" is beyond negation: not-two, not-that, without relativity, without comparison.

However, most *koan*s, and notably this one, have been used so much in Zen that they have lost their teeth to bite. Everyone repeats and repeats them until such *koans* lose their spontaneity; there is no life left. Having said that, everyone should study this exchange of Joshu's, research it and understand it for themselves. That is what I did; one day I asked myself this question: "What is this dog?" It is not a dog who barks. It is not a dog who bites; it no longer has teeth anyway. In any case, it is not the dog which matters here. It is the monk, that is, the mind of the monk who asked the question, which matters. However, everyone thinks about the dog. This monk was ripe and he was awakened, he understood and he certainly knew the *sutra* very well, in which it is said time and time again that "all existences have Buddha nature," even that of a dog. The monk could just as easily have asked, "Do *I* have Buddha nature?" Joshu would have replied in the same way: "*Mu.*"

These days this story makes us think a lot. Having said that, this observation in the *Nirvana Sutra* has never been made concrete, materialized or expressed and put into practice like it was at this moment. That was completely new. A *koan* was created at this moment—unconsciously and naturally, an eternal *koan*. A true *koan* is always eternal.

"Does a dog have Buddha nature?" Once someone replied, "Woof woof!" on all fours. How stupid! But what is the answer? You cannot answer intellectually with the frontal brain and this "woof woof" is only that.

The only response is faith—that is the response to all *koan*s, and no doubt, in the end, there is no need to deliberately use *koan*s, therefore no need to solve them either as Master Daichi said in one of his poems. If we prick up our ears and open our eyes, there is no need for *koans*; everything is there. That is zazen, the mind which functions without obstacle.

36. NATURE AND THE WORDLESS SERMON

The sun will always shine, the wind will always blow. Only sentient beings can look at the sun, feel the wind. But immediately human beings think they should classify it, place it somewhere in the cosmos, in the sky. And so they decide the sun is the central point. But it is only *they... we,* who say that. The sun is not the central point, but, just like everything else, only follows the cosmic system. Sometimes we think we can change the cosmos by artificial means—with barriers, dykes, artificial lakes, canals—but this is just temporary. In the end the cosmos, the eternal, the infinite returns to its original form.

I am always repeating, "You must follow the cosmic order." The true cosmic order is the Dharma. And the Dharma is not just what happens on earth, but what happens in all the galaxies.

The Dharma. Everything that exists manifests it, and not just in nature either. In Zen we often speak of the teaching of non-sentient beings, *mujo seppo.** Here is a poem by Master Daichi on this subject.

The wind disturbs the cold forest and leaves fill the garden
Even if there is no-one there, the outside wall has ears
Stone lanterns and columns, please
Do not raise your voice for a little while.

These non-sentient objects continually teach the law of Buddha, the universal law which exists everywhere: on this earth, on this planet, on other planets. This teaching is a teaching without words. It is not the teaching of a master or another human being. It is a sermon that never ends. The flowers, the trees, the stones, the tiles, the rivers all teach this law eternally. Many monks had *satori* while listening to the sounds of nature, the voice of the valley, the breath of the wind, or the murmur of a brook, the sound of a stone knocking on bamboo. Even while watching a peach blossom fall. This is the wordless teaching of the mountains, rivers and clouds.

In order to hear it, you must look at yourself from the point of view of the clouds, and for that you must become a cloud. That means without personal considerations, without emotions. If the wind blows from the south to the north, you go from the south to the north, if it is from the north to the south, the same. One *sutra* said: "Even if the eight winds blow, do not let yourself be moved." Do not run after things. Do not run away from things either. Do not be susceptible to criticism but look at everything from the highest point of view, from the point of view of the clouds, the moon.

That is death. Neither this nor that. The head of a dead person can understand *mujo seppo* easier than that of a live person. It is neither gloomy, nor dark, nor sad, it is great freedom. It is not determined by special forms; it is compassion beyond all that. It is beyond humanity. That means "compassion before"—primordial compassion.

Whenever the question of life and death was raised, Master Dogen used to say, "Ask the trees, ask the leaves!"[57]

And Master Deshimaru, used to say, "If you want to see our movement during zazen, you only have to look at the movement of the mountains." Perhaps that is also why he used to say that we must come back to the original point of human beings, before man, before woman, the place where the religious, spiritual mind expresses itself naturally and automatically.

Like I said before, *sanko* means life in the mountains, life in the forest. That is life during a Zen retreat. But that also means do not be led along by the forest, do not be led by the sounds, the blackbirds, the pigeons, do not be led by the wind, do not be led by the countryside,

57 "... you should ask the trees and the stones to proclaim the Dharma, seek out the paddy fields and the villages to hear their explanations, question the round pillars, study the walls and the tiles."—*Shobogenzo Raihaitokuzai.*

do not be led by the beauty of nature. Do not be influenced by anything. Do not lose the fact that you are yourself.[58]

Do not let yourself be infiltrated by nature, and remember Zen is not Taoism.* On the subject of Taoism, Master Nyojo said that it is a great spiritual path, which has influenced Zen enormously. But he added, "If you look at the moon, do not think of nature straight away." It is the same if you hear the sound of a bird. Do not think: "Ah that's a bird!" Do not listen to the birdsong with your mind. Do not create separations.

---

[58] You are you and no-one else. The donkey reflected in the water of the well, that is you. Having said that, your body, your form is not the reflection. In the *Hokyo Zanmai* Tozan said: "I am not that, but in fact that is me."

37. TRANSMISSION

It is not *something* which is transmitted. We say "to transmit," but in the end it is not transmitted. Rather, two minds come together—that of the disciple and that of the master. That is, if you will, "the awakening being awakened," not transferred. What is transmitted? My thoughts, my actualization, come from my master, but now they are being actualized through my disciples. By this actualization, I function in one way and you function in another.

When you do not follow your thoughts, you give without knowing it. On the other hand, if you follow your thoughts it is difficult to give. You add things up: "I've been practicing for so many years . . . ten . . . twenty years," and in the end you do not give anything. Elder practitioners do not calculate, should not add things up. They should always make room for others. That is the difference between elders and novices, the only difference: the elders give, since they have received. If they do not give, there would be no novices, only people passing through.

The first transmission in Buddhism took place on the Vulture Peak between Buddha, who turned the flower between his fingers, and Mahakashyapa who was the only one to smile at this gesture. This transmission has continued through the generations and the centuries till today. Kodo Sawaki received it from his master, even though, for one reason or another he never had the official certification on paper. He received that from someone else, a co-disciple after his master had died. Deshimaru was the same. He received the transmission from Kodo Sawaki, but he too did not have the paper certificate. He received the certificate from another master[59] after the death of Kodo Sawaki.

---

59 Yamada Zenji Reirin

This form of official certification has little in common with the smile of Mahakashyapa, and yet it is necessary, because without it the world would be full of false masters, charlatans.

Master Deshimaru on occasion would make fun of this officially certificated transmission.[60] All you had to do, he used to say, was to go to Japan, do a few zazens with the person from whom you wished to receive the certificate, perform a few impeccable ceremonies and a completely staged *mondo*, all prepared in advance.

One day, the Master staged this kind of theatre himself with a young Japanese monk. In the beginning, the *mondo* was quite normal, then the young Japanese, who was the head of a temple and already had the *shiho*,* got up and began to do a *mondo* in Japanese. He screamed and shouted. Then suddenly this monk rushed menacingly towards Deshimaru who was sitting on the high chair. I remember that we took it all very seriously, thinking he was going to behead the Master, so we were getting ready to intervene. He grabbed Sensei by the arms, pulled off his watch and threw it into the air with Japanese shouts all mixed in. Then Sensei struck him with his *kotsu*, the wooden stick that masters carry, and the other fell to the tatami. Everyone was happy! Then Deshimaru said, "There you are, that's the game. That's how they do it in Japan, and after that you get the *shiho*."

These days I do not think they still do it like that. But the problem these days is that you rarely know the master who gives you the transmission. You go over there, meet the head of a temple, pass through certain stages which last a few weeks, and do a *sesshin* adapted for foreigners, the *tokubetsu*, where there are only Americans, Germans, French who have come especially to receive the *shiho* from such and such a master. No-one is ever refused on condition that they have passed the stages A, B and C. After that you do *gassho:* "Thank you, thank you." Then you say goodbye: "Goodbye Master, see

---

60 The certified *shiho*

you soon perhaps." There you are, that's one form of master-disciple relationship.[61]

The *ketsumyaku* which is received during ordination represents the blood line, the thread which goes from Buddha through the patriarchs and masters. To be invited into or summoned to the master's room, for example, is of the greatest importance. It is often in this room that the essential education is passed between master and disciple. This is a unique occasion, when you receive true transmission, the true *shiho*. Some masters say that the disciple cannot receive the master's education in a room unless the master has slept there. That is how the transmission is received. The true *shiho* is simply one: master and disciple become one. There is nothing other than one.

That is the transmission. There is no longer any obscurity. It is *I shin den shin*, mind joins mind; the mind of the master, the mind of the disciple, just like the two candles on the altar: these two candles make one single light, and not only one single direction. The disciple's mind enters the master's mind like the lid on a box. It is not the master who is the box and the disciple the lid, just as it is not one of the two candles who is the master and the other the disciple. This however does not mean that the master and disciple are identical, they are different.

Master Sokei-An said, "My thoughts come from my master and now I transmit them to you. With these thoughts I react in one way and you react in another." I really like what Master Sokei-An says; he was a very free man. Also, he was one of the first Japanese masters to live in the United States. He died in 1945, just after having been freed from an American concentration camp situated near Washington. He died from the terrible treatment he received in that place.

However, one could ask why a master refuses to give the official transmission to one or another of their disciples. Master Ikkyu, for

61 In 2007, Philippe Coupey went to Japan to participate in the *Hossenshiki* ceremony at Tenryu temple. But the author knew Master Kishigami personally, his *shiho* Master, and he saw him regularly.

example, did not give it to anyone. Master Deshimaru did not give the *shiho* to anyone either. But does that mean that a disciple who has no written and stamped proof of transmission does not have a place in the lineage of patriarchs? Being in the lineage of the patriarchs does *not* depend exclusively upon having given the official certificate or not; it also depends upon what the disciples do after the master's death. If the master's teaching is strong and precise enough, it creates its own line, and it is the disciples who create it. It is always the disciples who create the lineage.

In the end, the line of transmission is the invisible which, little by little, engulfs everything. When people get tired of their own line, they run after grades, certificates. We get tired because we cannot see, cannot understand, the invisible in the line. (It is the same for whatever line one may belong to.) No need for a badge, no need to create an exclusive attitude; Buddhism, Zen, is not exclusive, it is not based upon prestige, it is not founded upon an accumulation of spirituality. That is not our practice; that is not our line.

All things have their invisible side which holds them and allows their transmission. Even the cement in the street which appears to be a crude and inert material is not that at all. Even this cement has its invisible nature, its cohesion...Making up a whole pile of stories about these lineages is not understanding something essential.

Our Soto lineage had a break between Master Kyogen* and Master Tosu*: Kyogen, whose name we recite in the list of patriarchs, gave the transmission to Tosu without ever having met him. That makes for an enormous dharmic drama which embarrasses many masters of the transmission. Master Dogen refused to talk about it, Daichi was not very clear on the subject, neither was Deshimaru who even used to say that Kyogen and Tosu met each other and that Tosu was even Kyogen's secretary! All this is impossible because Tosu was not even born when Kyogen died.[62] For me, the fact that they never met is not

[62] Kyogen died in 1027 and Tosu was born in 1032!

a great drama, since the line, as I have said, is imperishable, it *cannot* be broken: it has a natural, invisible, fresh, authentic and continuous connection, and too, its own élan vital.

There is something which is official and there is something which really happens; they are two different things. You could say that that has been the case for us since Master Deshimaru died. Even if officially things are not very clear, we should not have any worries about what to do, since the true line is very clear indeed. Not everyone shares this opinion. Some people say that the transmission from Kodo Sawaki to Master Deshimaru was not clear, and by conclusion that it never even occurred, and neither was it from Deshimaru to his disciples.[63] That is just one point of view, and an ignorant and therefore hostile one at that. For me, however, it is all very clear, as clear as it is dark at midnight. For some people it is light at midnight, while for others even midday is dark.

We have to understand that when a disciple is awakened, then everyone is. You only need one. Gutei's thumb, Unmon's stick goes beyond all the *sutras*, beyond all knowledge. Levels of understanding are different amongst disciples. "I only educate a few disciples," Buddha once said, "to obtain the highest goal I only educate a few. For the others, what can I do? I can only show the Way." Being the most awakened in the world or not, being the most advanced disciple or not, is not so important in the end. We can only follow the Dharma according to the circumstances of our own lives and of our own times, our very own era, now in the third millennium. We have to simply practice in our lives whether we are awake-awake or not awake-awake.

Amongst practitioners, each one blossoms thanks to the others; this can happen since we find ourselves on extremely fertile ground, and that ground extends too for those who teach. A teaching awakens

63 Now, if this were so, this would mean that we should no longer carry on in like fashion into the next generation.

something in another, a teaching blossoms, another blossoms...all the others blossom. That is how the *sangha* still exists.

And so, to come back to the beginning, what is transmitted? It is not something extra. Perhaps this sounds superficial, intellectual, but it is not at all. If you understand deeply with your guts that awakening is not something to obtain, you practice beyond duality, beyond all anxiety, beyond the personal, all those petty desires...without knowing it. So you see why it is important to understand with the body. What was your face before the birth of your parents, before the birth of Adam and Eve? Even before Adam and Eve this *nothing* was there.

38. DHARMA AND RELIGIONS

Master Eckhart said that, beyond God, there is the essence.

However, in general, religions have become really complicated. In Buddha's time you did not say "religion," as there was no name for it then, and all discussions in this vein were considered purely mental exercises. At that time, one spoke about "*dharma*" or "universal law." But mental activity has become really developed over time so that now we divide the *dharma* into separate compartments: philosophy, science, medicine, religion, and so on.

At that time, the *dharma* was perceived through the practice of *mushin*,* no-mind, not-thinking. But these days this way of expressing things disturbs most people. We associate not-thinking with ignorance, with primitive humans. "Not only could they not speak, but neither could they think. They were happy just making noises..." This way of looking at things is completely opposed to *mushin*, not-thinking.

Not-thinking is our inheritance. It is the transmission we have received from the primitive human. It has always been here and always will be, whether it is found within or outside of the *sutras*. Also, what we practice in the dojo did not begin with Buddha, but well before that, with original humankind. That is the *dharma*, the universal law.

Each school of Buddhism—Hinayana, Mahayana, Vajrayana*—claims to be the ultimate answer. Each one claims to come back to the original way of practicing Buddhism. It is always like that...and is completely normal; what *we* practice is the highest. If it were better across the road, it would be stupid not to go there. Just across the road from Fresnes prison is a café called *"Mieux qu'en face,"* "Better than Across the Road."

But in the end, all the ways are the same. Soto Zen, Rinzai Zen...I could even say that Christianity and Buddhism are the same. But you have to take just one path; if you take two you never make it. It is not a question of stopping your Zen practice to follow yoga or stopping yoga to follow Zen. It is a question of not following two paths at the same time, two different ways. Only one. But in order to follow only one, it is not necessary to stop all the rest—yoga, tai chi or any others.

It is interesting to note that, even though Shakyamuni* was the master and Mahakashyapa was his "closest disciple," the latter continued with a practice that was not really what Buddha had wanted to transmit. But it did not bother either of them. Mahakashyapa practiced a traditional Indian religion which gave birth to the Small Vehicle. Buddha taught what became Mahayana, the Great Vehicle. When Buddha died, it was Mahakashyapa who followed on. Whether it was Mahayana or Hinayana, Buddha had said to him nevertheless, "You are the same as me, Mahakashyapa...I give you half my seat." You are the same as me: you can educate others. Giving half of one's seat is a mark of great respect.

So let us not have preconceived ideas, let us remain open. Amongst the practitioners and *godos* in the Kodo Sawaki and Deshimaru lines, small differences have appeared in the teachings, and everyone thinks that they are doing better than the others. For some people the source is the traditional Japanese essence, for others it is the essence of Master Deshimaru's teaching. Some people have to go to Japan to the source, for others, the source is here within the teaching left by Master Deshimaru. It is as you like, perhaps this debate is necessary from time to time. When it is about the dharma, you need to be exact and calmly critical. On the other hand, it is not necessary to criticize others. You must know the difference between personal things and universal things. Unfortunately, people often make mistakes and the criticism becomes personal.

In any case, it is important not to have ideas about religion, about spirituality, like wanting to become perfect, for example. Wanting to become perfect is just an idea, and wanting to excel in religion is contrary to religion. Religion is not for oneself: it is abandoning oneself.

In this way, I made reference to Buddha once, saying that you must "kill Buddha." There are a lot of expressions like that to help us to understand and to advance smoothly on the great Way. Likewise, it is said that, "the *sutras* do nothing but harm to the human being." (However, you must not forget that poison can also become medicine.) Sometimes too, it is said that, "Buddha told nothing but lies" Of course he only told lies. Why? Because everything comes from *ku*, emptiness. All our thoughts, all my thoughts in any case, are false. I could quote lots of examples of things meant to free us from the obstacles created by humans. Buddhism takes away, takes away, takes away layer after layer. throws it all away. "You're a saint? Throw it away! You're Buddha? Throw it away!" And you might ask: In the end is Buddhism a good thing, this Zen practice? Yes, it is a really good thing, because in throwing everything away, you find nothing less than true freedom, deep and authentic.

One day, after having said that you must kill Buddha, I mentioned Mohammed, saying: "But above all *don't* kill Mohammed."[64] Afterwards, someone asked me if my remarks were a joke. It was not a joke, it was a teaching. That is the difference between Buddhism and other religions, whether it is Muslim, Christian or any other. Someone else said, regarding this remark about Mohammed, the *godo* should not talk about politics. *It is not politics!*[65] This is to make you understand that in Buddhism, and, above all in Zen, you must stop creating human fabrications around a word or an image which are only extensions of our small self. Our practice and that of millions of Buddhists throughout the world came into being for exactly this, to cease all human fabrication here and now.[66]

64 Philippe Coupey said in his teaching on Saturday 11th February 2006: "Please kill Buddha! I did not say Mohammed, but Buddha. Actually you should kill all these images, Mohammed's included. Kill the superfluous, kill the duality. This means find Buddha within yourself, find your original nature within yourself, not anywhere else."

65 In fact, Philippe Coupey was alluding to political problems raised at this time by caricatures of Mohammed published in the press.

66 Allow me to say, in the name of most Buddhist practitioners, that all these stories around "my Mohammed," "my Jesus" and finally "my God" have no religious dimension at all; they are based on dualistic concepts, completely childish, though violent and mistaken they are in the end, non-existent.

That is Buddhism: waking up to oneself and awakening others. We wake up to the present moment, the only reality, here, now. For that you must continually cast off other people's small egos as well as your own. Casting off your own small ego is not casting off your primitive mind—this mind which existed before the birth of your parents. This mind is never disturbed.

Master Senzaki*[67] simply said that, "Buddhism is giving and forgetting." He also said, "That is the way to maintain the *sangha*." Senzaki was a monk who refused all positions, he did not want the official transmission. He did not want a fixed place, he regularly changed where he practiced, which he called "the floating dojo." He taught in the United Stated before and after the two world wars and he died in 1958. Today, American Zen Buddhists have difficulty placing him, because not only did he refuse all structure, but neither did he try to get the *shiho*, the official transmission. He spoke very unfavorably of this transmission in the 1920s, saying that no monk, no master, should certify him, Senzaki, in any lineage after his death. He also used to say that a true Buddhist never preaches. In this vein he would say, "I have never asked you to come to this place. It is your own Buddha nature that brings you here." These are words we no longer hear today. He used to say to his disciples, "If you want to practice zazen, if you want to take the vows, the ordination, so that you can observe the *kai*, the precepts, I will ordain you monk or nun, and I will try hard to live a Buddhist life by your side." And again, "No guest in our house (our dojo) should occupy himself with spreading the teaching, or even preserving the movement. A Buddhist should dedicate his time to meditation." That reminds us of Bodhidharma. And Senzaki also said, "My wish is that you all practice true Buddhism, you follow the discipline of Zen monks and forget your mundane conditioned opinions."

Become light, without any weight, spiritual or religious, on your shoulders.

---

[67] Nyogen Senzaki, 1876-1958

A disciple handed me a poem one day, though I don't know by whom:

Walking with a light step
Buddha's earth does not stick to your sandals.

That's it. Do not be attached to Buddhist concepts, do not be enslaved by the *kai*, do not want to obtain *satori*. No weight on your shoulders, no Buddha's earth stuck to your sandals.

39. TRUE COMPASSION

In Zen, we insist on working with the frontal brain as little as possible. It is often because of this part of the brain that we experience problems. The idea, for example, of wanting to help the whole world can lead us to hell. Religions are always saying that we should help others, yet they cannot stop creating war amongst themselves, here, there, everywhere. I need not list all the conflicts connected with one religion or another that poison our society. People say, "What I do is not about me, it's for *my* religion." But "my religion," it is always *me*; religion is just a ruse to hide the "me" behind it. At the same time, when it is the "me" who gives, this is not necessarily true compassion.

Take for example, the tsunami that struck in the Indian Ocean in 2005. Because human beings are gregarious animals, everyone wanted to send millions of euros to the victims. Everyone is touched in a different way about this or that event, of course, but what you should really touch is what you have in front of you. Unfortunately, this is not the message relayed by the screens and media about the tragedies that happen on this great earth. It no longer touches people that a neighbor has just been killed by the thief next door. It is no longer about the homeless who wander in front of the dojo at rue Tolbiac in Paris.[68] They live locally and they need money, but that does not count, that is not politically correct. We will help people on the other side of the world, instead of helping those who are right in front of our noses.

Obviously, we must help people by every means possible, but not in order to feel good afterwards. In truth there is no measure, there is nothing that one *should* give, nor something that one *should not* give. It is not a question of giving a *fuse** beyond your means. For example, to think, "I don't like the idea of giving to those who do not

---

68 There stands a big building, next door to the dojo, which houses people without lodgings, ex-prisoners on state probation and so on.

work," is simply not being ungenerous but completely ignorant. You should feel the primordial kindness which is within yourself as in all others. Then you give when you give, and you do not give when you do not give. And so when you give, even if it is only five euros, you are happy to give these five euros knowing that it comes from something profound. And giving fifty euros does not change anything...even one euro is enough.

Really giving, what is that? Really giving is giving wisdom to others. It is to lessen their suffering through the body and mind rather than through the wallet. In this way, over and above the pecuniary aspect, bodhisattvas elevate themselves, but also descend into illusions in order to save, or at least to help other beings, other existences. Kodo Sawaki said that in practicing you must go back down to society. "We are always in the process of climbing," he would say. "You have to go down from zazen to help save the world. Rise up to attain *satori* and go down to save beings from suffering." In a poem, Daichi told how "stupid Gautama," that is Shakyamuni Buddha, "could only increase his ignorance" by always rising up, climbing the mountain of asceticism. He had to come down too.[69]

You can help materially—go to Africa, give food, treatments for HIV; it is absolutely imperative to do things like that, but this is neither climbing nor descending from the mountain. It is not necessary to go out into the street with ideas of wanting to help in order to descend from the mountain. Even if it is said in Buddhism that we are there to help others, Zen does not think like that, does not work like that. Bodhisattvas do not think they are helping, do not think they are giving, do not think of themselves. They simply use the means at their disposal, without thinking in any particular way about it.

In Buddhism there are a thousand Buddhas. The bodhisattva Avalokitesvara is the twenty-fifth. Avalokitesvara, Kannon in

---

[69] Taken from the poem n° 6 *Shusan no so* by Daichi. (The silhouette coming down from the mountain.) *Poèmes de Daichi commentés par Maître Deshimaru*, volume 1, p.37 (AZI, 1994).

Japanese. In the *Hannya Shingyo* which we recite every morning in our dojos, the first word is *Kanjizai** the bodhisattva Avalokitesvara. Avalokitesvara means "to observe freely"—to look at yourself, to look at others freely, which means not to get stuck on ideas, concepts. And then you can understand that even a dirty street can teach you; and not just teach us (us men and us women), but also the animals (plants, if there are any in the street). There are dustbins. What do the dustbins teach us? Everything teaches us. A lot of Zen poems talk about that: the teaching of non-sentient beings, the teaching of the dirty street.

"Garbage can, oh my beautiful garbage can."

In truth I think that this mind which we develop unconsciously is much more compassionate than the idea of "wanting to help others." I often have exchanges with my disciples on this subject, of always wanting to help others. The idea of helping others implies that there are others, and that the others are in need of help—double mistake. By this linear way of thinking you create people who are in need. That is not the mind of the bodhisattva; the bodhisattva does not think in terms of helping others, and in that way does not create people in need.

That is why we sometimes hear phrases like, "There is no-one on this earth for us to help."[70] That is great compassion. We are the only ones who can help ourselves.

---

70 Taken from the poem Hotei Osho (n°10) by Daichi. *Poèmes de Daichi commentés par Maître Deshimaru,* volume 1, p.49 (AZI, 1994).

Here is a poem by Master Toan: "The clouds do not depend on the *sutras* of Guatama in order to climb in the sky."[71] How do we help our original nature? It has no need of help…*Hishiryo*, that which shines during zazen, and not just during zazen. Even if Buddha's mind is covered with dust and completely submerged by phenomena, it is always connected to the cosmos. No purity, no impurity.

Yes, through the practice of zazen we know that within the mountain a diamond is hidden. It is brilliant, it is clear, but there is no need to pamper it, caress it, to love it and think, "This is mine." Not at all. You must break it, attack it with a single strike like the strike of the *kyosaku*. That is the only way it will expose its secret power. And what does that mean? It means do not become attached and it will show itself. That is true for all things.

Do not be attached. You must break it, that is, go beyond it. Do not fall into the trap of, "I have something to give you," or "I am a bodhisattva, I have something to give, and I give it to *you*." If you give something it is because it has been stolen, it does not belong to us, it is not yours to give. It is presumptuous to think that we can give anything.

71 "The clouds climb the sky without a staircase/ But they do not lean on the *sutras* of Guatama," Teshima Toan, 1718-1786.

Primordial Love

Not the waste waves and their weedy gulf-streams, shalt thou take for guidance: thy star alone,—"Se to segui tua stella!" Thy star alone, now clear-beaming over Chaos, nay now by fits gone out, disastrously eclipsed: this only shalt thou strive to follow.

—Thomas Carlyle, *Past and Present*

True compassion means helping others to cut their karma. Teaching them to listen, to hear and see things as they truly are. For this, a gentle approach does not always work. Sometimes brutal tactics are necessary. Shock turns everything upside down for them and changes their actions.

Compassion is not a question of some outward show, but rather an inward fire that each of us can feel inside ourselves. This fire exists and has existed since before the birth of our parents. It will still exist after the birth of our children. We might know it as the "primordial source" or even "maternal love."

One wonders if we will ever be capable of changing our karma, our crimes, our tortures, our brutality towards men, towards women, towards children. Religion has not been able to obtain such results, even less so politics. But this is of little importance, for one who knows their purpose in this world pursues it without worrying so much about the outcome. When one person improves their karma, the karma of the whole world is affected. Obviously this goes beyond what we can intuitively understand about our karma. Karma concerns actions, their causes, and their consequences.

Buddha himself explains that it is not the individual who pursues path or rebirth, but it is the act itself that is repeated. That is to say that if one were to die in kamikaze action, this destruction would repeat itself eternally, like a free particle that ricochets on the surface of the water in constant renewal.

The understanding of Buddha, and of his manner of explaining karma, aims to liberate human beings, not to imprison them. This understanding is illustrated in the story of Yuse, who had sexual relations with a married woman. Because the husband found out and was embarrassed and enraged, Yuse killed him. Plagued by enormous guilt and remorse, Yuse then turned to the teachings of Buddha and became a monk. This taught him the emptiness of everything.

Emptiness—a state constantly on the verge of becoming a potential, is inherent in everything.

Yuse understood this teaching, profoundly.

At the moment the spirit rediscovered its original purity, there was no more sin. It is not that the sins never existed, but we are no longer able to locate a trace of them.

Yuse is no longer guilty.
He is neither guilty nor innocent.[72]

This passage symbolizes the great compassion of Mahayana Buddhism which is based on a conception of the world called *sunyata* in Sanskrit, *ku* in Japanese, and *vacuité* (emptiness) in French. It teaches that sentient beings and insentient objects are not fixed entities but a composition of many impermanent components. What is a tree? The trunk, the roots, the leaves, the rain, the wind…? The origin of these manifestations or components can be found in what Deshimaru called the fundamental cosmic energy. This energy manifests itself in an eternal renewal which we can observe in the four seasons of the year. One could say that Yuse, in our example, has returned to this fundamental energy, emptiness.

He deeply understood that we are all linked to and never separated from the same fundamental energy. Even the act of murder is, in the end, included in this highest reality.

Using your bodily posture and your breathing, you can directly influence the mind, unconsciously and automatically. Here, respiration plays a critical role because it irrigates the brain. Respiration is what allows you to refresh the brain and to constantly renew the circulation of blood. Body and mind become strong and balanced.

He who knows how to breathe and to look himself in the eye realizes that he no longer needs to run away. Rather than fleeing, he empathizes directly with what makes us suffer so much.

72 See "The Song of Awakening" by Kodo Sawaki.

Suffering can be beneficial and allow us to embark on the path to liberation.

Suffering bears witness to a certain nobility. It is not necessary to flee what is noble.

This is how we heal ourselves—and the entire world—automatically and unconsciously.

One can heal in this way the mental illness, the conflicts, the ignorance, and the illusions of society and of the world.

Because karma influences all of us,
each and every one of us,
and deeply engraves its mark,
on all people everywhere.

All of us, however, are raised from a young age in the spirit of competition and must bear its fruits: fear, persecution, paranoia. From the beginning to the end of our lives. School? Competition. Sport? Competition. The very meaning of sport is relegated to the background; it is only important to win.

For months one can watch nothing but the Olympic Games. A runner who has trained twice a day, three hours in the morning and three in the afternoon, for twelve years finally wins a medal, but it's only bronze. He weeps in front of the cameras! He wanted nothing more than to win silver.

What a waste of time for humanity.

In spiritual practices you can see the same scenario. Martial arts used to be a spiritual practice. It involved killing a man, oneself. Now, it exists solely to beat the opponent and take home a medal.

In the path of Zen, you find the same thing: competition.

When we are exposed to this kind of weakness, we should be glad because it gives us something to observe, to act against, to transform.

Whenever anyone manages to trade their desire for honors and social status for the path of the cosmic order, then everyone can be happy.

Excerpted from *Fragments Zen: Mémoires de chair* by Philippe Rei Ryu Coupey, translated by Richard Collins and Isabel Collins

40. INTERDEPENDENCE

When someone speaks, someone else listens. When one person shouts, someone else receives the *rensaku*. When the president on the other side of the Atlantic drinks, the prime minister on this side becomes drunk. When one person awakens, another person awakens, whichever side of the Atlantic they are on. Each one of you can understand this. If a *Rinzai* monk manages to solve a *koan*, the *Soto* monk has *satori*...

41. AWAKENING

From far away it shines within me. *Satori* comes from afar. It comes through the ancestors, through the Buddhas of the past. There is a tendency to think that *satori* comes from within ourselves, but why would it come from ourselves? It does not come from us, it comes into us from outside. We do not create *satori* by practicing zazen, we do not create *satori* by our concentration—but yes through our concentration. Whether we are in the dojo or not, we open ourselves to *satori*. That is *genjo*, materialization of phenomena. Whenever we abandon our small self automatically and unconsciously, truth comes our way. That is *genjo*.

The moon, amongst other things, is the symbol of awakening, of *satori*. It comes from far away, from outside of me, of you, of us, it shines within me, within us.

There are all kinds of *samadhi*. There is Zen *samadhi*, Buddhist *samadhi*, the *samadhi* of Buddha, all of that is quite similar: it is to hear, to think, to practice. Having said that, it is not the same *samadhi*, the same awakening as in other religions, not at all. For example, Ramakrishna,[73] when he was in *samadhi*, stayed for days with his mouth open, so that the flies could go in and out. That is not the Buddha's awakening, it is not our practice of *samadhi*. Our *samadhi* is the same whether we are in meditation or not.

Samadhi, is completely being. The awakened person, I think, is one who is completely conscious of what she or he is doing. She is conscious that she is in zazen, she is not in a mystical state; she is not in some other place. Conscious of the body, the hands, the back, the back of the neck, the chin. He is conscious of his breathing. Even though he does not follow his thoughts, he knows that he is thinking.

---

[73] Indian sage (1836-1886)

If the awakened person is not conscious that she is thinking, she can never live or know non-thinking. When Dogen wrote the *Shobogenzo*, he was awakened, I assume. As was Master Deshimaru when he educated his disciples. And when they practice zazen there is no difference. Why should it be different? It is a state which is both normal and incomparable at the same time.

However, this awakening, which is freedom, can be the very thing that enchains us. Wanting to get *satori*, Daichi called that the "golden chain" in another of his poems. True, there are all sorts of chains; wanting to be His Majesty, or something like that, for example, is a silver chain, but is a chain nevertheless. In the end, what is the difference between a golden chain and a chain made of a base metal? What is enchained is enchained, whether it is in a monastery, a palace or a factory, it is all the same.

The golden chains bring with them the same suffering as the desire for nice material things. We think that the desire for non-material benefits is more evolved, but in the end it is worse, since being attached to the non-material means you are fooling yourself as well as others.

Satori means cutting the chains. The great *satori* is the final hall, the perfect hall, the radical hall, the hall of completion.

Kodo Sawaki used to speak of the incomplete: "We carry something unfinished around for a long time, and we console ourselves by saying that it is the same for everyone. This is what I call mass madness. We think we must be like other people." That is not *satori*. *Satori* is creating your own life. Kodo Sawaki added: "That means waking up to the mass madness."[74] Those who create their own lives understand that there is nothing to lose. Or perhaps they have everything to lose, their illusions as well as their wisdom. At this moment you can really let go.

---

[74] *To You*, Kodo Sawaki, (Hohm Press. 2021)

Skateboarder, Place de la Bastille
"Satori is to create one's own life."

We create all our chains ourselves, not others. Even a prisoner is not really limited by the size of the cell. One day Waldo Emerson[75] the American Transcendentalist went to visit H. D. Thoreau who was in prison.[76] Emerson said, "But Henry, what are you doing behind

---

[75] Ralph Waldo Emerson (1803 – 1882): Founder of Transcendentalism in the United States, a movement of religious philosophy.

[76] Henry David Thoreau (1817 – 1862): essayist and American poet, he declared himself to be morally above the law—and that was why he was in prison, in this case for refusing to pay taxes supporting the Mexican war. He was a partisan of the passive resistance movement and known for living according to a moral code superior to the written law (see his "Civil Disobedience," 1849). His work had a great influence on the passive resistance movement led by Gandhi in India, and on the Civil Rights movement led by Martin Luther King.

those bars?" And Thoreau replied, "Hey Waldo, what are *you* doing in front of them, tell me that?"

All of that is illusion, bars, chains—we are all conditioned. Whether we are conditioned by a dictator, conditioned by the mass madness or conditioned by the desire for *satori*, it is all conditioning. Whether it comes from outside or inside, in the end it's always inside. If not, we could not say we are born, we live, we die and nothing has happened; since nothing will have happened.

42. HERE AND NOW

Nothing ever really happens because fundamentally time does not exist. To not create time is to not follow your thoughts. Not to create thoughts is to not create causes and effects. If you let everything go, everything that rattles around in your subconscious—thoughts, desires, feelings, wishes, regrets, and finally all mental designs—inevitably the past will no longer have any importance, no longer any power over you. And if the past no longer has any influence, then the same goes for the future, as one cannot exist without the other, and one cannot disappear without the other disappearing too. Of course, everyone comes to zazen because of their past or even because of their future. But zazen is beyond all timetables. Zazen is the practice of great freedom, here and now. Then there is no birth and no death. You could even say "no coming into being" or again, "no becoming, only being."

In order to function in the world, we think that each day follows another, but there is no first day, there is no second. If we think that there is a first and second day, we will never be able to find the original substance. This is not easy to explain, but I am sure that someone practicing for some time will understand what that means. Do not fall back into the ordinary way of seeing things where everything is carefully arranged...with a period of time divided into what we call the "four seasons."

On this subject, Master Deshimaru said something interesting like this: "Keep control of yourself, see that the springtime is already established in the heart of a harsh winter." What he wanted us to understand is that we should not be perturbed by changes, they are always there. Everything is in the moment, there is no before or after. At the moment when a phenomenon arrives, it is already disappearing. There are never moments without changes.

In the chapter entitled "Uji,"* Master Dogen says that the present moment is not found in the dimension of "time and space" and that time and space reveal but the dimension of "cause and effect." In scientific terms we talk about the fourth dimension; you need very high-level mathematics to explain it, like Einstein did. In Zen we explain that by practicing zazen, which is awakening, beyond our small self, beyond unilateral thought, past, present or future, which is only a concept based on appearances and not on true reality. True reality is not found in any doctrine of time and space. Time and space is but a human creation.

In the end, how can you be any happier than in the present moment? It's not even necessary to be beyond happiness, unhappiness, because, as has just been mentioned, this happiness is only a concept, only a memory. The present moment is neither happy nor not happy. It is a matter of what you are, which is *ji juyu zanmai**[77]; you are the joy which cannot be expressed, beyond words.

And the present moment never passes. Where could it go?

---

77 *Ji juyu zanmai*: the *samadhi* of your own joy that no-one else can understand.

43. IMPERMANENCE

Paradoxically, everything is in movement: the waves of the sea or the snow settling, everything is changing, inside, outside. Phenomena are forever changing. We can see it in our own lives, but also in other people's lives, in the environment. We are nothing but change. Change, movement.

From a very young age we notice that everything changes perpetually. The monk, the nun, the bodhisattva, the sincere practitioner of the Way has to observe *mujo*, impermanence. "You should always observe *mujo* without wasting any time," Dogen said in his *Zuimonki.** The mind of awakening, *Bodaishin,** is the mind that observes *mujo*. Everyone who follows the Way must observe *mujo*.

Later, with maturity and life experience, as I said before, you also notice that if in fact everything changes, then quickly you notice, you realize, that nothing changes. Change is only apparent and found at the level of form. If we can understand that *everything* is change, movement, then we can also understand that nothing changes. *Mujo* alone does not exist; for in the end, the body is indeed permanent, the *Dharmakaya*, the body of the practice, the body of Buddha. So those who practice the Way sincerely have nothing to worry about on this subject. There is only here and now.

44. DEATH AND REINCARNATION

People suffer when faced with death. Seeing our close ones die makes us unhappy, and we are also unhappy when we have to die ourselves. Generally, we are not all in such good health, and if tragedy comes, that is the moment when we touch the bottom; that is death. It's just like that: *mujo*, impermanence. "In any case we cannot stay here," said Michel Bovay, one of Master Deshimaru's closest disciples, just before he died. We cannot keep this body forever, this ego to which we are so attached.

Ki, as you know, is the oxygen in the air and food, which is transformed into human energy. Having said that, this energy needs a channel in which it can exist. We are like bubbles: we keep a certain form for a short period of time, a form which reflects everything, or which should do so, if the bubbles are not obscured by illusions. And then, one day, they burst and disappear for good. When we lose the channel, the body, *ki* goes somewhere else of course. And so, at the moment when *ki* changes its place, we can no longer remain.

The elements which constitute the body return to the four elements of the cosmos. This is Buddhist teaching. Flesh returns to earth, blood returns to water, heat returns to fire, breath returns to air. And so, we can see that the universe depends upon us just as we depend upon the universe. We are the universe, we are the world, and death is absolutely essential, since the universe could not exist without it.

We can see our own death like that: our life comes to an end and so also our own cosmos. However, if we have not been able to settle this question of life and death, our illusions will continue even though we are dead. That is transmigration, reincarnation; it is returning to the wheel of life and death, *samsara*.* It is not the self in particular who comes back; it's an energy which continues, the energy of our actions, whether they be physical, verbal or mental. To die, our own death, is not important at all. I think that what is important is the state of mind at the moment of death. You really have to pay attention to the karma you are creating and have created. At the moment of death, consciousness separates from the ego and returns to the *alaya* consciousness, the universal consciousness, and the karma, the seeds of karma we have created return to their latent state. These seeds manifest themselves and materialize on the earth amongst men and women, and also amongst the gods and *deva*s.* That is why it is important to do a ceremony for the death of those close to you, to help and influence the seeds of karma which come back and will keep returning forever.

If a person dies full of obsessions, the person does not come back but their obsessions remain behind for others to deal with, if they can. This is what is reincarnated. So, it is not for nothing that we are born as we are. The same goes for suicide. We think we only have to die in order to solve our problems, but that is too simple. If that were the case there would be no need for Buddhism. But the problems continue, they are transmitted and reincarnated, and this is where Buddhism comes in. For instance, to think that the body is our own is a false notion. We do not possess the body, the body "is" that is all. The person who commits suicide thinks that their body belongs to them. Like all of us, they are stuck in the illusion of "my" and "mine." Thinking that jumping in front of a train will destroy this illusion is wrong; in order to destroy this illusion you have to have a spiritual practice.

The Tibetan Buddhists take suicide very seriously. In cases of suicide they do a lot of ceremonies to protect future generations and to protect those close to the person, the victim, here and now. No-one is alone, we are all totally interdependent. We are all in the same family. So suicide continues, it is reincarnated. The same goes for the actions of a person like Buddha as much as anyone else. They carry total liberation. Those who meditate in a cell like the Tibetans, or those who practice zazen in a dojo, change the whole world, not just here and now, but in the future, and even in the past.

And so it is necessary to have a deep understanding of reincarnation, of transmigration. In Buddhist teachings, things are not unilateral, locked into categories. Here and now is the past, present and future in its totality. Reincarnation is living here and now: you are what you are. You are everything. Everything is here. You do not become something. Wood does not become ash when it is burnt. Wood is wood and ash is ash. It is always in the present moment. If you believe in reincarnation in the sense that wood becomes ash, then that is mere belief, and that is not understanding that attachment, here and now, is in itself a reincarnation.

"What was your face before you were born?"[78] Is this question resolved at the moment of your death?

Errol Flynn, the famous actor of the 1940s who was a friend of my father's, was at a party when he collapsed. When he realized that he was about to die his last words were: "Good God, is this all there is to it?" This is certainly a valid question for all those who have never practiced the Way: "Is this all?" He died of surprise.

When Master Takuan died, on the other hand, his last utterance was a single word, "dream." Takuan could not talk of death when he said "dream" because he wasn't dead yet, and he did not want to talk about something he didn't yet know. But his disciples had come to him with pen and paper: "Write something!" How annoying they were! Bothering the master when he was in the process of dying, and only in order to hear such strange things as "dream." He could have said the opposite, "life is not a dream," and it would have been just as pertinent.

In any case, faced with death, it is certainly not knowledge that matters, nor our successes, our material or emotional achievements in life. Certainly, faced with death, what comes to mind is not what we have in the intellect, in the frontal brain, but what is in the

78 The *koan* is usually, "before the birth of your parents."

hypothalamus, the deep brain (which means, incidentally, that part of the brain which is used for the practice of zazen). Faced with death, does having been president, for example, really matter? That cannot be taken into the coffin with you. You could even ask yourself: "During the time that I was president of this country did I really make good use of my time?" I think that, as far as individuals go, of course, someone who has practiced zazen can say for certain that the time spent in zazen was not wasted, that that time was used completely and totally. But to have been president...?

It is often said that zazen is to see the dead man's point of view. Going into the dojo is just like stepping into your coffin. This is not sad or morbid; it simply means setting aside your personal baggage; thoughts of good and bad, right and wrong. That does not mean that you have to sit like a dead body of course. If you are dead, you cannot let your thoughts go, you cannot stretch the spine, tuck in the chin and breathe long and deep, and so develop a *hara* which is strong and natural. If you are dead, you cannot stretch the bow; that is to say, have a strong tonus. If you are dead, you can no longer make your illusions disappear, and so reach awakening. You can no longer deepen your faith, your holy and religious mind.

We always speak of impermanence, of change. And even if our own cosmos disappears when we die, we must not forget that there is also permanence. One cannot go without the other. That was why the Buddha, as a young man, set out on his quest; he saw the sufferings one experiences on the death of someone close. As I was saying, everyone, without exception, is unhappy at that moment; we touch the depth of unhappiness. That is why the Buddha set out to find something greater than all the ideas and all the practices that existed at that time. And what did he discover? That not only the mind, but the body is also permanent. That is *Dharmakaya.* That is the deep realization that life and death are as one.

So let us wake up! Wake up! Before our flesh returns to the earth, before our heat returns to the fire, before our breath returns to the air, before our blood becomes the rain again. Of course, and apart from all this unhappiness, it is still a good thing that we die. And this is so for all of us, for every living thing. Otherwise, there would be no fire, there would be no air, there would be no earth, there would be no water, there would be no universe... There would be no water falling like rain from the clouds. If there was no death, there would be no source. There would be no furious thunderclaps to break apart our sleeping minds.

The Lightest of Light Wind Passes

To leave something behind, to make a change, it is necessary to have energy. Otherwise we wouldn't even be able to turn around, stuck always in outdated mental constructions.

It is not so much we who create this vital energy as it is the vital energy that creates us. Depending on how we receive this vital energy, also called *qi*, we exert more or less power over our lives.

We inherit a certain *qi*, transmitted by our ancestors, which diminishes as we age. But there is also the *qi* we acquire; this is the *qi* that interests us.

How can you develop a powerful *qi*?

Acquiring a powerful *qi* is necessary, if only so that you are no longer influenced by toxic environmental elements such as the media and its false promises.

If you live in comfort and material wealth, it is obvious that your *qi* will be weak. Everyone can understand that. But some think that for the *qi* to be strong it is necessary to be a samurai, tough and ascetic. This is not the case. On the contrary, it is possible to be soft and mild and to develop a strong vital energy. One can be both delicate and have plenty of *qi*. In other words, sweetness has nothing to do with weakness.

Others think that peaceful people, those who are not as busy as machines all day and who prefer to daydream while gazing out the window, have a weak *qi*. This is another error. Rest has nothing to do with softness.

The Way of the samurai, the Way of combat, is called *budo*. Notably, this term is composed of an ideogram which means "to go forward with the spear," which clearly demands *qi*.

An ancient manuscript on budo addresses this question of *qi*. The author, Chissai, explains that when *qi* becomes weak, sicknesses appear. He says that *qi* often finds itself weakened by a cold wind or humid heat. At any rate, one who has weak qi can easily fall ill. So can someone who is too sensitive, always worried, or overly susceptible to favorable and unfavorable environments.

This manuscript also speaks about how in the art of budo,

or martial arts, energy can find itself hamstrung by thinking. So someone who has bound-up *qi*, or *yin*, will be slow wielding a sword, which is not a good thing when faced with an opponent intent on slicing your skull in two. And so you should avoid finding yourself tied up by your thoughts.

On the other hand, when *qi* becomes predominant, too lively, *yang*, or burned out, you lose yourself in a nervous energy, superficial and inconsistent. When this happens, you will be swept away by your opponent *"like dry leaves swept by the wind."*

Qi should be developed through simple movements. During zazen, of course, you do not move. The body does not move, but neither is it rigid. There is instead a continual movement that is unique: a movement of the mind. This movement is without beginning and without end, like a river. There is no movement simpler than this.

What is truly necessary is the heart. The heart and vital energy are fundamentally One. For *qi* to be exact, authentic, unconscious, natural, and automatic, we must have a heart that is transparent, which obscures nothing. Such a heart is the embodiment of direct communication from one person to another, heart to heart; nothing can come in between.

It is all about the breath. The oxygen we breathe is transformed into *qi*.

Lightly, lightly, very lightly
The lightest of light wind passes
And away it goes ever so lightly,
I don't know what I'm thinking
Nor do I wish to find out.
And I don't know what I'm thinking,
Nor do I wish to find out.

—Fernando Pessoa

Excerpted from *Fragments Zen: Mémoires de chair* by Philippe Rei Ryu Coupey, translated by Richard Collins and Isabel Collins

45. FAITH—ACTUALIZATION

One day in Master Nansen's* temple, an argument broke out about a cat. To whom did he belong?

Nansen arrived at that moment and asked: "Does this cat have Buddha nature or not?" This is how it is written in some texts. According to other sources, Nansen said: "Give me a Zen word otherwise I will kill the cat!" But it comes to the same thing, something had to be said in reply—a single word, a single gesture, but precise enough and capable of exhausting ourselves in the ten directions.

"If no-one answers I will cut the cat in two!" The monks were quite surprised; this was not Nansen's style. He was a severe master, especially when it concerned the *kai*, the precepts. You didn't eat garlic, you didn't eat fish, you didn't eat meat, all this food was forbidden in his temple. So, he was hardly likely to kill a cat. Why Nansen would not even allow mosquitoes to be killed, not in his temple anyhow.

But no-one could say or do anything, they were all afraid. Afraid of what? Afraid of winning or losing the cat? So they all tensed up. Don't think about winning, don't think about losing... but act! However, those monks in the temple didn't do anything, so Nansen killed the cat and everyone was horrified.

Once the cat was dead, Nansen was alone in his room and Joshu, his closest disciple, came to see him. "Good evening master! You do not look so well today."

"Yes, I've just killed a cat."

He told him the whole story. "If you had arrived earlier Joshu, what would you have replied?"

Joshu took off a sandal and put it on his head, turned around and left the room. At that moment Nansen said to him: "If you had arrived earlier I would not have had to kill the cat."

All human beings and all other creatures are here to help us awaken. And "us" does not just mean we human beings; it means the entire universe—cats, flowers, cattle, fathers and mothers. We need to have a great and compassionate vision, not a conventional point of view which says that it is wrong to kill a cat, but to see and understand through a primordial compassion. The cat was not there for nothing, it was there to awaken us till this day. It woke me up, that cat. I thank it; this cat has created great merit. But, beware. Did Nansen really kill the cat? All those stories are just fingers pointing to the moon, not the moon itself.

In the end it's a question of faith. By faith we understand that we are born on this earth for one single reason: to awaken ourselves and to awaken others. It is for that reason that we are always talking about coming out of *samsara*, the wheel of life. In other words, avoiding perpetual reincarnation, avoiding living with the conventions of the time, of the era—as in the Middle Ages when all black cats were killed because they were believed to be bewitched. Conventions are just conventions, we have to have undying faith, and not just faith in ourselves or the masters of the transmission, but also faith in human beings, and even more than that, faith in one's own nature, the original nature. Then we can see things with the eye of faith, understand things with the mind of faith.

Faith without object is one that dwells on nothing, and so faith brings us to actualization. It is not actualization that comes from faith, but faith which is realized by actualization. You also know that faith is neither logical nor rational, and not the opposite either. It is not something that must be understood at any price.

Freedom. That is what I am talking about when I talk about actualization. Actualization is what is lived in fact. It is freedom, *par excellence*, of the human being and by the human being; so, in actualization we lose ourselves. Actualization and faith become the same thing.

In other words, actualization is never something we become, we have become, or we will become. It is a question of trust in oneself, not trust in what we have been or could become, but trust in the fact that "we are," that "I am," that "you are." This is how we can understand faith.

46. FREEDOM!

It is important to ask yourself this question: Why practice zazen? Is it for yourself? Is it to follow a tradition from elsewhere? Is it to follow that which is universal? A *sutra* says: "In this world you will find no way to save people." The only way is to discover *Maka Hannya,* the highest truth of our lives. Life, our life, without separation. And what is the highest truth which is not Buddha or God? When faced with death, perhaps we will have a reply. At our death, which is not really the end of our life, we could ask ourselves what has really been important in our lives here on earth. At which moment have I lived completely, totally?

I think we do zazen to transform ourselves. To change, to cut our karma. And in transforming ourselves we transform the whole world. It is said that one person practicing zazen can change the whole world.

If we practice exactly we can change ourselves deeply, beyond forms and categories. But what does that mean, to practice exactly? It is a question that is asked more and more, particularly these days. But the answer cannot come from yourself because in the end there is no self. You must reach your own conclusions.

Master Deshimaru, for example, while he was a monk in Japan, concluded that he must leave his country, because over there Zen Buddhism had become "pure formalism." Those were his words. Even zazen was only a part played in this formalist gathering. "That is why I came to Europe," he used to say," to plant the seeds of true Zen, just zazen, in this fresh earth." Does Master Deshimaru's conclusion concern us today? Is it also ours, or simply his? You alone can decide.

Whatever you decide, it only takes one thing, one sword to cut through the *bonno*s, the illusions. And for that it needs to be a well-sharpened sword. The zazen that we practice was not created by Buddha, it has existed since time immemorial. When we understand our own zazen, we can understand the zazen of the mountains with brilliance. That is *komyo*, the marvelous illumination. It shines, it has always been shining with brilliance since time immemorial.

Our teaching, our practice, is to always go forward without interruption. Straight in front of us as if we were alone on the earth. That means not to be distracted by what we see with our eyes, what we smell with our noses, what we hear with our ears. But to go forward without interruption, even during sleep. In truth we have no choice because in any case everything changes, and because of that we have to become completely present at every moment in our lives.

Just as we are alone in our lives, at the moment of birth and the moment of death, from moment to moment, from birth through to death, so also are we not alone. We are alone, but we are with others; we are completely intermingled and interdependent with all other creatures. Just as Kodo Sawaki said, when we desire something, we desire with the whole world. The same with stealing, lying...desiring awakening. If you get lost, you get lost with everyone, the whole of society. If you do zazen you do it with the whole of society.

And so we should not let ourselves be led by our mental difficulties, our personal sufferings, emotions, material problems, our inability to succeed in society, even though we have great talent and abilities. In the end, these are just waves that ruffle the surface of the ocean.

One master wrote, "The shadow of the bamboos sweeps across the steps, but not a single speck of dust has moved." And here is another way of saying it: "The shadow of the bamboos in the moonlight has swept the dust on the steps all night, but nothing has happened." There you are, not a speck of dust has moved. We are born, we have lived and we die, and nothing has happened. That is the bottom of the ocean, the bottom of the sea.

Make room. Empty out your personal mind, throw out your ideas, your anxieties, your bitterness, your suffering, our suffering. Make room for God or Buddha who is nowhere other than within our selves. And that "we" is not the froth, it is the belly of the ocean. We human beings are different from animals. Since, even though the human being comes from the earth just like everything else, it goes towards the sky, it opens out to the cosmos. We come from the muddy earth, from the muddy waters of consciousness and we grow up like the lotus flower opening out into the heavens. We have come here on this earth, we have lived and we have died, and nothing has happened.

To blossom like the lotus flower born in the mud, we must not have any baggage, neither for nor against. No need to be attached to any particular color. Do not be a prisoner of your own personal thoughts and then you will always stay in the middle of this lotus flower. You always see Buddha in the middle of the lotus flower in

Gardens of the Sacré-Coeur, Montmartre

"We must not have any baggage."

statues, in pictures, in *thangkas*. He is not sitting on anything hard, not on a rock or a peak. He is not practicing asceticism. He is sitting on something soft—that is his teaching. Soft like a *zafu*.

Softness is not weakness. Softness supplies the necessary connection so that energy, *ki*, can circulate—a *ki* which enables impetus, spiritual impetus.

What does Buddhism bring? It is a question that has travelled through the history of Zen. Monks and nuns always ask this question. But they cease to ask it when they become mature in the practice of zazen. We know of course that Buddhism brings us nothing at all. It is only after fifteen, twenty years of daily practice that the monk can say: "Yes, in effect, nothing happens. Yet I am completely satisfied. This 'nothing' is more extraordinary than I ever could have imagined. Extraordinary. Marvelous! I am free!"

GLOSSARY

Alaya, (Skrt): "Storehouse consciousness" or that which is common and pre-exists in everyone. It contains the true seeds of each "body-mind" when it is incarnated by the process of birth.

Ananda: One of Buddha's principal disciples. He served for twenty years under Shakyamuni and then twenty years under Mahakashyapa. It is said that his exceptional memory enabled him to retain all of Buddha's teachings, which was of great value later when he played a central role in the compilation of the first sutras. Zen regards Ananda as the second Indian Patriarch.

Arhat, (Skrt): Someone who has reached a very high degree of accomplishment in Hinayana Buddhism. By following the precepts and the practice rigorously, he or she has attained enlightenment.

Avalokitesvara, (Skrt) (Jap. *Kannon*): "The lord who looks down from above" or "the one who hears the supplications of the world." The *bodhisattva* of infinite compassion, Avalokitesvara is often represented with eleven faces and a thousand arms in order to respond to the sufferings of all beings.

Bankei (1622-1693): One of the more popular Zen masters in Japan. He contributed strongly to the revival of Rinzai Zen which was continued by Hakuin.

Baso (709-788): Disciple of Nangaku and Master to Hyakujo, Nansen, Daibai Hojo and the secular layman P'ang. Patriarch of Rinzai Zen known for his lively methods of education including shouts, rough gestures and strikes with a stick, meant to awaken the discriminating mind of his disciples.

Bodaishin, (Jap): The mind of awakening. The mind that aspires to the highest dimension of the Way. The mind that observes *mujo*, impermanence.

Bodhi-tree, (Skrt): The tree under which the Buddha had the experience of awakening, after forty-nine days of sitting meditation.

Bodhidharma, (4th-5th century. Jap: Daruma): Disciple of the Indian Master Hannytara and Master of Eka. He is the first Patriarch of Chinese *Ch'an* Buddhism, and the twenty eighth in the Indian line which is uninterrupted from the time of Buddha. It is said of Bodhidharma that he was the son of a Brahmin from Southern India. He immigrated to China where he re-centered Buddhism back to zazen rather than the exclusive study of the sutras. It is said that he practiced for nine years in a cave near the Shaolin monastery on Mount Suzan. Hence his nickname, "The Brahmin facing the Wall."

Bodhisattva, (Skrt*)*: "To be enlightened." Everyone can reach self-realization and dedicate their lives so that others may also be enlightened. Such is the bodhisattva vow to participate in the social reality. Nothing distinguishes them from others and yet their mind is "Buddha."

Bonno, (Jap): "*Bon*" means that which troubles or disturbs, and "*no*" means the cause of suffering, of torment. *Bonno* is generally translated as "passions" although that term is a little too restrictive. *Bonnos* are illusions, attachments and all the products of the personal consciousness. To go beyond them makes up part of the four bodhisattva vows. (*See* Shiguseigan).

Buddha, (Skrt): "The awakened one." Written with a capital letter, means the historical Shakyamuni born in Kapilavastu in 536 BCE and died in 483 BCE. In addition, there are also: (1) The legendary Buddhas of the past present and future. (2) An individual who attains awakening. (3) Enlightenment or Awakening. (4) "The Principle of Buddha," the fundamental cosmic power and/or the true nature of the universe which manifests itself in different forms.

Buddhism: "The Religion of Awakening," one of the great spiritual and philosophical of human directions. It was founded in the 5th century BCE by the historical Buddha Shakymuni. It is divided into two main branches, Hinayana and Mahayana. Hinayana, commonly known as "Theravada," is spread throughout the Indian mainland through to Sri Lanka, Burma, Thailand, then to Cambodia and Vietnam. Mahayana spread from northern Indian to Tibet, Mongolia, China, Korea and Japan, but equally to Vietnam where the two branches co-exist. Kodo

Sawaki said; "Buddhism is simply a question of knowing how to live this life for its greater good, how to live a life that makes sense."

Ch'an, (Ch): *See* "Zen" (Jap).

Daichi Sokei (1290-1366): Japanese Zen master known for his poetry. He received his monk's ordination from Kangan Gin (1217-1300)—a disciple of Dogen who later practised with Keizan for seven years. At the age of 25 he went to China where he stayed for 11 years. On his return to Japan, he received the transmission from Meiho Sotetsu (1277-1350), one of Keizan's successors.

Daisai geda puku, "takkesa ge," (Jap): The Kesa sutra. Mainly chanted three times after the morning zazen. It is a reminder, especially to those who wear the Kesa (the garment given at monk's or nun's ordination), that to follow the teachings of Buddha contains and extends to all things.

Dai sai geda puku / Muso Fukuden e / Hi bu nyorai kyo / Kodo sho shu jo.

Daishin dharani, (Skrt, *Usnisa Vijaya Dharani)*: Known as the sutra "Of great compassion." It was translated many times from Sanskrit into Chinese between the 7th and 10th centuries, when it was then brought to Japan. Today it is mainly recited for the sick and the dead.

Deshimaru, Taisen (1914-1982): Disciple of Kodo Sawaki and great Japanese Soto Zen master who spent the last fifteen years of his life teaching in Europe. He received monk ordination as well as the robe, bowl and spiritual transmission from Kodo Sawaki in 1965. In 1975, while he was teaching at the dojo that he had founded in Paris, Deshimaru received the official *shiho* from Yamada Zenji, abbot of Eiheiji. In 1985, Niwa Zenji, abbot of the same temple, conferred on him the posthumous title of *Zenji*. Deshimaru founded more than one hundred dojos in Europe, North Africa and Canada, as well as the temple of La Gendronnière in the Loire Valley. According to temple records he ordained more than 500 monks and nuns, and over 20,000 people practiced with him at one time or another. His teaching comprised nothing special. He was content to teach zazen, the same zazen practiced by Bodhidharma, Eno and Dogen, without adding anything or taking anything away. He taught nothing other than sitting, with no personal modifications; long, deep breathing, and the mind of samadhi, the self beyond categories that he called *hishiryo* consciousness.

Dharma, (Skrt): The fundamental law, the universal order as it is shown in the Way. But also it is the teaching, the Buddhist doctrine, as given by the historical Buddha Shakyamuni.

Dharmakâya, (Skrt): The body of the *dharma*, the aspect of Buddha which is beyond form and manifestation. This state of emptiness, where one's true and absolute nature is found, is *zazen.*

Diamond Sutra, (Skrt, *Vajracchedika-prajnaparamita sutra.* Jap, *Kongo kyo):* Autonomous part of the Prajnaparamita-sutra which is of central importance in the Buddhist teachings of the South-East Asian countries. This sutra teaches that the manifestations of phenomena are not reality, but are just illusions, the projections of our own minds.

Dogen (1200-1253): Great Japanese Soto-Zen Master, disciple of the Chinese Master Nyojo and Master of Ejo. He developed Soto Zen in Japan and founded the Eihei-ji temple situated in the mountains to the north of the country. He came from a family of high nobility and studied Rinzai Zen and the use of *koans* according to the teachings of Masters Eisei and Myozen before going to China where he met Master Nyojo who gave him the certification three years later. Dogen is author of a major work, the *Shobogenzo,* in which most of his teachings can be found. The teachings of Dogen revolved essentially around three points: The practice without goal or objective (*mushotoku*), the abandoning of body and mind (*shin jin datsu raku*), identifying practice with awakening (*shusho ichinyo*).

Dojo, "do," the way, "jo," the place, (Jap): The place where we practice.

Dokan, (Jap): The Ring of the Way. The continual repetition of life's everyday acts in full consciousness. Repetition of the posture, and the attitude of body and mind when in uninterrupted practice (*gyoji*)

Dokusan, (Jap): Private and formal interview with the Master, during the course of which the Master evaluates the depth of understanding of the disciple by using *koans*. Dokusan is principally practiced in Rinzai Zen.

Doshu, (Jap): How the Way is experienced or how the understanding of the *dharma* is manifested in each individual. The expression of the Way through body, speech, consciousness and behavior.

Eiheiji: "The monastery of eternal peace" (Jap): one of the two principal monasteries of the Soto Zen School, the other being Sojiji. Founded by Master Dogen in the 12th century, it is situated in the north of the central part of Japan in the Fukai province, well known for its harsh winters. The name Eihei given by Dogen corresponds to the year (67 in our era) when the Indian monk Matto brought Buddha's 42 sutras from China for the first time. Today Eiheiji is the headquarters of Soto Zen which has 15,000 temples both in Japan and elsewhere.

Ejo, (1198-1280): Principal disciple and secretary to Master Dogen. Known for his fidelity to his Master (whom he helped to build the first true Zen monastery in Japan), as well as the historic work he undertook by transcribing and compiling the *Shobogenzo*. He met Dogen in 1234 at Koshoji temple, became his disciple and remained at his side until the Master's death in 1253. He was the second abbot of Eiheiji and his only written work was *the Komyozo Zanmai*. At his death he requested that his ashes be buried beside those of his Master in the place reserved for the secretary.

Eka, (*Huike*, 487-593, Ch): Disciple of Bodhidharma and second patriarch of the Zen lineage. It is said that, in order to show his desire to be accepted as a disciple, he cut off his own arm. He stayed with his master for nine years simply practicing *shikantaza*. After receiving the transmission, Eka went to live in the city where he managed to work as a road sweeper while teaching the *dharma*. He was 100 years old when he died—a victim, according to some sources, of an assassination plot by the local chief of police for having aroused jealousy among certain powerful Buddhist priests.

Ekô, (Jap): Chanted dedication of the meditation and the sutras which are recited at the end of zazen. In the mornings it is usually dedicated to the ancestors of the lineage, as well as those assembled for zazen, to all existences, and in certain particular cases to people who are sick or who have died.

Eno, (*Hui-neng*. 638-713. Ch): Sixth patriarch, disciple of Master Konin (*Hung-jen,* Ch). Eno played an important role in the spread of *Ch'an* in China. According to tradition, Eno was illiterate and was awakened when he heard a monk reciting the Diamond Sutra. His thoughts and influence are described in what is known as the "Platform Sutra."

Four noble truths: The essence of Shakyamuni Buddha's teaching expressed in four points. The truth of suffering, the truth of the origin of suffering, the truth of the extinction of suffering and finally the truth of the practice that leads us to the extinction of suffering. (The eightfold path).

Four vows, (Jap, *shiguseigan*): The Four Great Vows of the bodhisattva. They are recited after zazen in dojos and monasteries everywhere.

However numerous the beings, I vow to save them all.

However numerous the passions I vow to vanquish them all.

However numerous the dharmas, I vow to acquire them all.

However vast the Way of Buddha, I vow to realize it.

Fukanzazengi, (Jap): "Universal rules for the practice of zazen." The first text that Dogen wrote in 1227, just after he returned from China.

Fuse, (Jap). (*dâna*, Skrt): Giving, alms. The spontaneous giving to those close to us, of material things, of energy or wisdom. One of the fundamental Buddhist virtues. One of the six "ways of perfection" (*paramita*).

Fuyo-Dokai, (Jap) (Furong-Daokai, Ch) 1043-1118: Chinese Zen Master of the Soto lineage, famous for having watered down the soup whenever his disciples increased in number. Born in an era of relative decadence in Zen, he restored it to life in its original purity. Dogen said of him: "He is the source of Soto Zen, its roots, its branches, its bones and its marrow." Often quoted by Master Deshimaru, Fuyo-Dokai used to say:" Do not allow your daily life to run after your own gains, do not take an interest in your own health. Cut off your two heads as well as the one in the middle."

Gasshô, (Jap): "Palms of the Hands joined together." A gesture of reverence and respect, the hands joined at about 10 cms. from the face, the tips of the fingers at nose-height and the forearms horizontal. The left hand symbolizes the spiritual world and the right hand the material world or phenomena. Therefore, *gasshô* represents the unity of the spiritual with the material, the sacred with the secular, and the human with God, the cosmos.

Genjo, (Jap): Spontaneous manifestation of things as they are.

Genjo koan, (Jap): Title of the first chapter of Dogen's *Shobogenzo* composed in 1233. This text is thought of as the backbone of his teaching. It speaks essentially of the relationship between the practice and the realization of ultimate truth. Therein are found various famous parables like the ones about the moon and its reflection, the wood and its ash, and the bird and the fish, as well as the famous maxim; "To study the Way, is to study yourself."

La Gendronnière (Zen Temple of): Situated in the Loire Valley in France and founded by Master Deshimaru in 1979. Principal temple of the *sangha* of Master Deshimaru's disciples (recognized by the Japanese Soto Zen authorities). Niwa Zenji went there in 1984 to give official certification to three of Master Deshimaru's disciples, Roland Rech, Stéphane Thibault and Etienne Zeisler. Outside of the traditional summer camps lasting two months, there are courses, symposiums, lectures and other activities linked to Zen Buddhism. But La Gendronnière is, above all, a place of practice, dedicated to *sesshin*, daily *zazen* and *samu*.

Ginsberg, Allen (1926-1997): American poet and founder member of the Beat Generation. His poetry, an example of the Beat Generation itself, is characterised by its freedom of tone, and its deliberately disjointed form, and is linked to spontaneous writing. The "Flower Power" slogan used by the Hippie community was attributed to him.

He travelled extensively (notably to Mexico, India, Japan, China and Cuba) and was close to Timothy Leary (the advocate of LSD) and to Chögyam Trungpa Rinpoché whose disciple he became in 1970.

Godo, "the back room" (Jap): One of the two sections of the meditation hall in Japanese monasteries. Designated to the more senior monks to whom would fall the responsibility of "surveillance" in the dojo. In Europe, the godo is the monk or nun who is responsible for giving the teachings and who directs zazen, although not necessarily recognized as a "Master."

Gutei, (Jap): (Jinhua Juzhi, 810?-880, Ch). Disciple and successor of Koshu Tenryu. Gutei became well known for the *koan* about the thumb. When anyone asked him a question he simply raised his thumb in the air. When he was at the point of death he spoke to his disciples, saying: "I have received the Zen of Tenryu's raised finger, and I have applied it inexhaustibly throughout life."

Gyoji, (Jap): Continuous practice, eternally without beginning or end. Maintaining the practice in all actions, remaining in *dokan*.

Hakuin: (1686-1769). Japanese Master of Rinzai Zen considered the father of modern Zen, because of the reforms that he imposed and the energy with which he infused this school, which was in decline since the 14th century. He systemized education through the use of the *koan* and he emphasized the importance of zazen. "What is the sound of one hand clapping?" is one of his more famous *koans*. He was also an accomplished painter and calligrapher.

Hannya shingyo, (Jap): (*Maha Prajna Paramita Hridaya*, Skrt). The Sutra of Great Wisdom also known as the Heart Sutra. It is chanted in all Zen temples after zazen. This very short Sutra expresses the "heart" and the essence of Mahayana teaching on *ku* (emptiness).

Hara, (Jap): The center of vital energy also known as the *Kikai Tanden*, situated just below the naval. In Zen as in the martial arts, the energy free from tensions and personal will is concentrated and manifested in the *hara.*

Ha-shang Mahayana: (8th century). Disciple of Kataku Jinne who himself was a disciple of Eno. He was a Chinese Ch'an monk in the tradition of Immediate Illumination. He was invited to Tibet by King Trisong Detsen to establish the Samye monastery. He had to leave quickly after being defeated in a philosophical duel with the Indian Kamalasila. Through this duel he was obliged to recognize that the gradual way was also valid. Historically, the consequence was that Tibetan Buddhism was created with a gradual Hindu influence.

Hinduism: Hinduism is a religion made up of a set of beliefs, rites and precepts, revised in the 3rd century BCE, supported by *sanatana dharma*, "the universal cosmic law with no origin." To obtain liberation (*moksha*) from the cycle of reincarnations (*samsara*) constitutes the ultimate goal of all its philosophies and its mystic Indian techniques.

Hinayana, (Skt): The Small Vehicle. This term has a derogatory connotation, used by the followers of Mahayana Buddhism to describe the Buddhist trends which seek liberation for all individuals from *samsara*. It is equally known as "The Buddhism of the South" because of its geographic establishment in South-East Asian countries (Sri Lanka, Thailand, Burma, Cambodia and Laos). It is based by and large on an ideal of purity, the extinguishing of passions, attained by following a strict moral code. Its ideal is the figure of the *arhat*. Today it is represented by current Theravada which describes itself as the original Buddhism.

Hishiryo, (Jap): Beyond thinking and non-thinking. This means thinking at the depths of non-thinking, beyond the personal consciousness, to abandon the mental process which builds up in the frontal brain and to think with the body. *Hishiryo* consciousness appears when the personal consciousness follows the cosmic consciousness. It is the essence of the practice of zazen. Along with *shikantaza* and *mushotoku*, *hishiryo* constitutes one of the three pillars of the teaching of Kodo Sawaki and Taisen Deshimaru.

Hokyo Zan Mai, (Jap): "Samadhi of the Precious Mirror." This poem from Zen Master Tozan (died in 869) is one of the four essential, ancient Zen texts together with the *Shinjinmei*, the *Shodoka*, and the

Sandokai. In the word "Soto" used to designate a school of Zen, the "to" refers to Master Tozan and the "so" most probably refers to one of his disciples, Sozan.

Hotei, (Ch. Pu-tai), died in 916: Chinese monk whose name means "the hemp sack" since he always carried one on his back. Legend tells us that at his death his true identity was revealed: he was an avatar, an incarnation of *Maitreya*, the Buddha of the future. His image has been reproduced as a laughing Buddha, which can be seen in many Chinese monasteries today.

Honen, (Jap) 1133-1212: Founder of the Japanese Buddhist School *Jodo-shu*, "The Pure Land School." The practice of *Jodo-shu* consists of reciting the name of Amida according to a ritualistic formula: "*Namu Amida Butsu*" (in the name of Amida Buddha). The goal is to be reborn in the pure land of the Buddha Amida.

Hossu, (Jap): "Broom for chasing away small animals."About 30 cms. in length, the *hossu* is a kind of fly-whisk with a bunch of horse or yak hair at one end. Each Master would pass their's on to a disciple.

Hyakujo, (Jap): (Ch. Baizhang Huaihai) 720-814. Disciple of Baso and master of Obaku. Known today, amongst other things, for his famous *Shingi*, Monastic rules. One quote composed shortly after his death says: "On all the earth, the Ch'an schools have followed his example like the grass bending under the rain." Moreover, he insisted on the important link between the practice of zazen with the daily work to be carried out in the monasteries and the fields (*samu*), and it is to him that we attribute the famous Zen saying: "A day without work is a day without eating." Hyakujo was one of the most remarkable Ch'an masters of the Tang dynasty and he taught the *dharma* for more than 40 years.

Hypothalamus: The central, instinctive, primitive brain as opposed to the frontal, rational, intellectual brain.

Inmo, (Jap): *See* "suchness." *Inmo* is also the title of chapter 17 of Dogen's *Shôbôgenzo*.

Ikkyu: (1394-1481). Rinzai Zen master, poet and calligrapher. Often referred to as the "practical joker of Zen" on account of his non-conformist way of life, Ikkyu is certainly one of the more popular Zen characters in Japan. Like a mad saint he stigmatized the decadence of Rinzai Zen in the big monasteries. Ikkyu would often call himself "mad cloud" or even "blind donkey." His poems honor the great masters of ancient times, deplore the decline of Zen and sing the praises of wine and carnal love. In 1474 he became abbot of Daitoku-ji, one of the great temples to which he was connected, but continued to lead his life with no less freedom from constraint. He took care not to designate any successors.

I shin den shin, (Jap): A fundamental notion in Zen which describes the transmission beyond the written word and intellectual understanding, from heart-mind to heart-mind. From the master's mind to that of the disciple. It was Kodo Sawaki who, one day, used this expression "from heart-mind to heart-mind." The phrase was first used by Eno the 6th Patriarch.

Jijuyu zanmai, (Jap): The *Samadhi* of Zen. It is the fourth principle of Dogen's seven principles. *Jijuyu* means to accept, to receive for oneself; *zanmai* means *samadhi*. Master Deshimaru explained it in this way: "*Samadhi* is received by oneself alone. We can experience joy by ourselves, others cannot understand it. The *samadhi* of Zen is *hishiryo*. *Hishiryo* is the true *samadhi*, authentic joy."

Joriki, (Jap): Physical power. Strength or power particularly as a result of the concentration developed through the practice of zazen. Joriki provides a constant presence of mind and a capacity always to respond to circumstances appropriately.

Joshu, (Jap): (Ch. Zhaozhou Congshen) 778-897. Great Zen master, disciple and successor of Nansen. Master Dogen called him respectfully "Joshu, the old Buddha." Even though he had thirty successors his line was extinguished after a few generations. There are a few well-known *koans* that evoke the character of Joshu, in particular: One day a monk asked Master Joshu, "Does a dog have Buddha Nature?" and Joshu replied "Mu" (nothing).

Kai, (Jap): (Skrt, *shila*): The precepts or disciplinary rules. In Zen the ten *kai* are the rules of natural morality that the disciple receives from the master on being ordained a monk, nun or bodhisattva. "Receiving the *kai*" *(jukai).*

Kali-Yuga, (the age of, Skrt): Translated literally as the age of the demon or the age of vice. It is what is known as one of the four ages which divide time in the sentient world, according to Hindu cosmology. It should be pointed out, that the present age we are now living in is indeed the Kali-Yuga, the Dark Age.

Kan, (Jap): The great vow, as made by all the Buddhas and Bodhisattvas. Profound aspiration for the practice of the Way, and the transcending of the self.

Kanji, (Jap): original Chinese characters used in Japanese language together with *kana* which make up Japanese syllables.

Kanjizai, (Jap): the first word of the sutra *Maka Hannya Haramita Shingyo*, the heart sutra. The name of the bodhisattva Avalokitesvara which means "the one who looks down," who is the Buddha of compassion.

Karma, (Skrt): "Action." The law of universal causality. The totality of our actions and their consequences. *Karma* is created through body, speech and mind. *Karma* is the law of cause and effect and from it comes transmigration and *samsara* (the cycle of rebirth).

Ketsumyaku, (Jap): Certificate of affiliation to the lineage of Buddhas and great masters, from the past up until ourselves, which is received at ordination.

Kesa, (Jap) (Skrt, *keshaya*): The Monk's robe. A grand garment made up of many pieces of material carefully assembled together, worn by monks and nuns draped over the left shoulder and on top of the *kolomo*. Given by the master during ordination, the *kesa* is an object of faith and veneration. It symbolizes the transmission, and the belonging to the uninterrupted lineage of Buddha's disciples, an existence in a dimension which transcends the small ego.

Ki, (Jap) (Ch, *chi*): According to the Taoist idea it is the vital energy, the life-force, the cosmic mind that penetrates and animates all things. In the human body it is in the region of the naval (*kikai tanden*, "ocean of breath") where *ki* accumulates. By extension, it is each Zen master's way of teaching.

Kinhin, (Jap): Slow walk, in rhythm with the breathing, practiced between two zazen sittings.

Koan, (Jap): Literally, "Public case." Phrase, word, act or gesture that brings one to an understanding of the truth. Equally an instrument in the education of disciples. Rinzai Zen uses *koans* as a technique to abandon mental states. Soto Zen, which attributes no value to particular states and identifies *satori* as the normal condition, does not use *koans* to train disciples. The *koan* represents, as much for Soto as for Rinzai, a paradoxical aspect, the contingency of reality.

Kolomo, (Jap): Black robe of the Zen monk or nun, distinguished from the kimono by its large sleeves and worn over a white or grey kimono.

Kotsu, (Jap): Stick measuring about 30 centimeters given to a Zen Master by their own Master. It is formed with a slight curve like the human spine.

Ku, (Jap): (Skrt, *sanyata*). Often translated as "empty" or "emptiness" as opposed to *shiki*, phenomena. However *ku* and *shiki* are one. *Ku* represents the infinite, the non-birth out of which all that is born or finite proceeds or returns. This is the place of transformations. This is the origin, the common identity without which differences (phenomena) could not exist. *Shiki sokuze ku, ku sokuze shiki*, phenomena become (are) emptiness, emptiness becomes (is) phenomena. Emptiness is form, form is emptiness.

Kusen, (Jap): Oral teaching given in the dojo by the master during zazen. Teaching which addresses itself directly to the deep consciousness of the practitioners without passing through the intellect. It seems that *kusen* is specific to the lineage of the Masters Kodo Sawaki and Deshimaru. Most other lineages prefer talks, *teisho*.

Kyogen, (Jap): (Ch, *Hsiang-yen, Chih-hsien)*, died in 898. Disciple of Isan Reiyu. Intellectual and great erudite who studied closely with Hyakujo, but never managed to understand his teaching intimately. For this reason, when Hyakujo died, he followed his co-disciple Isan.

Kyosaku, (Jap): "Stick of Awakening." Stick which is used to strike the shoulders of practitioners during zazen. (More precisely, on the trapezium, the muscular region between the shoulder and the neck). Generally given at their request. The *kyosaku* is a means by which practitioners are helped to come back to the normal condition, by dissipating drowsiness (*kontin)* or calming agitation (*sanran).*

Mahâkâshyapa: 6th century BCE. One of the principal disciples of Shakyamuni Buddha, known for his self-discipline and strict morality. He became head of the *sangha* after Buddha's death. He is considered to be the first patriarch of Zen Buddhism.

Mahâyâna, (Skrt): "Large Vehicle." One of the two branches of Buddhism, the other being Hinayâna, "Small Vehicle." Mahâyâna appeared in the first century BCE. Its aspiration is to free all beings by going beyond the liberation of the individual. This attitude is embodied in the Bodhisattva, the one who takes the vows whose principal virtues are compassion (*karuna*), and the development of the mind of awakening (*bodhicitta*). Principally established in Tibet, China, Korea and Japan.

Mondo, (Jap): Questions and answers between master and disciple to deepen the understanding of the *dharma*. These sessions of questions and answers in the dojo provide an opportunity to clarify pertinent questions about life and death according to the practice, not in a private and intimate discussion with the master as is the custom in the Rinzai school (*dokusan*), but for the benefit of the public assembly of the sangha.

Mu, (Jap): Prefix which signifies "nothing," "nothingness," "none." Nothing, but not in the sense of the opposite of something. *Mu* is more than a negation; it implies an absence. It can be found in a number of Japanese expressions like *mushotoku* (non-profit), *mushin* (no-mind) and *muga* (non-ego).

Mudra, (Skrt): "Seal." Gesture or position of the body or a part of the body. It is usually a reference to the hands or the fingers whenever their position takes on a symbolic or ritualistic meaning.

Muga, (Jap): (Skrt, *anatman*). Non-self, absence of ego. The principle of non-identification with the ego, in terms of a separate existence and an individuality of spirit.

Mujo, (Jap): (Skrt, *anitya*). Impermanence. One of the three characteristics of existence, along with suffering (*dukha*), and non-self (*anatman*). The observation of *mujo* is an essential aspect of the practice of the Way. Master Daichi wrote: "*Mujo* never ceases to spy on you. It only takes a moment, and it will hit you, and with such a speed and brutality that you will be thunderstruck before you have even realized it."

Mujo seppo, (Jap): The wordless sermon. This is the teaching given by non-sentient beings (the river, the mountain, etc.), by Nature.

Mushin, (Jap): No mind, without personal consciousness. State of consciousness without dualistic thinking, the cessation of discriminatory thought, when the mind is not fixed.

Mushotoku, (Jap): Without desiring profit, without goal. *Mushotoku* refers to practice without an object, without a goal. It is about giving without expecting any return. Master Deshimaru used to say that it was this fundamental aspect of Zen which brought him to the practice.

Muso, (Jap): Non-form. No appearance; that which is beyond appearances.

Nangaku, (Jap): (Ch. Nan-yüeh Huai-jang), 677-744. Zen Master, one of Eno's principal successors, and master of Baso. He was the precursor to what later became Rinzai. (Seigan, also one of Eno's disciples, became the precursor of Soto.)

Nansen, (Jap): (Ch. Nanquan Puyuan), 748-835. Disciple of Baso and Master of Joshu amongst others. Seven years after his master died, he isolated himself on Mount Nansen where he practiced zazen for 30 years. Then he spent the last ten years of his life in a monastery, surrounded by over a hundred disciples.

Nagarjuna: (2nd-3rd century). Indian Buddhist philosopher, founder of the Madyamika School ("the middle way"). He was the fourteenth patriarch in Zen Buddhism, after the historical Buddha. Well known for his teachings on the doctrine of *ku (sunyata* in Sanskrit: emptiness), which he developed from studying the *Prajnaparamita* sutras. According to the legend from which he gets his name, he searched for these sutras in the underwater kingdom of the Nagas (serpents) and transmitted them with the accuracy of an *arjuna* (archer). He is therefore traditionally represented with one or several cobras creating a kind of umbrella above him.

Nirvana (sutra of): (Jap, *Nehangyo*). Shakyamuni Buddha's sutras, exhibited just before his death, describing the events relating to his entrance into nirvana. They emphasize the true nature of the Self and the eternal presence of the state of Buddha in all things.

Nyojo, (Jap): (Ch. *Tiantong Rujing)*, 1163-1228. Disciple of Setcho Chikan and master of Dogen. Soto master of the Sung dynasty who was installed as abbot in the Tendo monastery in Southern China and taught only zazen. Resolute adversary of "spiritual syncretism," he concluded that the unique teaching of Bodhidharma needed nothing amalgamated nor added. Nyojo was the last of the great Chinese *Ch'an* masters. It is thanks to Dogen who brought his teaching back with him to Japan, that it is perpetuated until today.

Patanjali: (Around the 1st/2nd century BCE). Founder of the philosophy of Yoga, presumed to be the author of the *Yoga-sutras*.

Paramita, (Skrt): Generally translated as "perfection," the term *paramita* (*haramita* in Japanese) represents the six qualities practiced by the Bodhisattva: *dana*, giving, charity; *shila*, morality; *kshanti*, patience; *virya*, energy; *dhyana*, meditation; *prajna,* wisdom.

Platform Sutra: Sutra attributed to Eno which constitutes the fundamental text of Southern Ch'an known as "the school of immediate illumination." In this text it is taught that Awakening can be attained by grasping immediately the emptiness of our nature and of all phenomena.

Rakusu, (Jap): Small five-band *kesa* worn around the neck, and also used outside of the practice room. Whereas the large *kesa* is reserved for monks and nuns, the small *kesa* can be worn by those who have not only received monk ordination, but also the bodhisattva ordination.

Rensaku, (Jap): Series of strikes with the *kyosaku* on the muscle between the shoulder and the base of neck, administered by the master or assistant. Used to revive the concentration of the whole *sangha* when a serious error has been committed.

Rinzai (school): School founded in China by master Rinzai in the 9th century. Today it is the principal school of Zen along with the Soto school. In Rinzai, they make more formal use of *koans*; and zazen, which is practiced facing the center of the dojo, is considered a method for attaining *satori*.

Rinzai: (Ch. Lin-chi) ?-866. Zen Master, disciple of Obaku (Ch, Huang-po). To train his disciples Rinzai used methods which appear to destabilize the ordinary consciousness; such as abrupt shouts of "Ho!," brusque strikes with either the stick (the *shippei* or the *kyôsaku*) or the fly whisk (*hossu*).

Ryôkan, (Jap): 1758-1831. Zen monk, hermit and poet. Ryôkan followed the teachings of Kokusen for twelve years, whose "seal of confirmation" he received. Following Kokusen's death, Ryôkan embarked upon a long five-year pilgrimage across Japan. He ended up by settling in a hermitage on Mount Kugami not far from his birthplace, where he dedicated his time principally to the writing of poetry, many examples of which are considered to be the most beautiful in Japanese literature.

Ryutan, (Jap): (Ch, *Longtan Chongxin*), 9th century. Disciple of Tenno Dogo and master of Tokusan. It is often told how, after a long conversation that went on into the night, he said to Tokusan, "It's getting late." On lifting the blinds to leave, he was faced with complete darkness, so he asked his master Ryutan for a candle. However, the latter blew it out as he gave it to him. Tokusan bowed, having been deeply struck by this gesture, he said, "I will no longer doubt the words of the master."

Ryuzan, (Jap): (Ch, *Yinshan*), 740-830. Disciple of Baso. He spent his life as a hermit in the mountains.

Samadhi, (Skrt): (Jap, *Zanmai*). State of meditation, and of the availability of the consciousness during zazen. Pure awareness, unconscious and without object. Master Dogen said: "The s*amadhi* of the Buddhas and patriarchs is frost and hail, wind and light."

Samsara, (Skrt): (Jap, *shoji*). Cycle of transmigration of the soul and of existences (birth, death and rebirth) conditioned by attachment. The opposite of nirvana even if, fundamentally, they are not separate. Composed of the six realms of existence which make up the dispositions of the mind: *shomon* (human), *asura* (warrior), *deva* (god), *chikuso* (animal), *gaki* (hungry ghosts), *naraka* (hell).

Samu, (Jap): Period of collective work usually carried out in silence, like cooking etc.

Sandôkai, (Jap): "the fusion of difference and similarity." Poem by Master Sekito Kisen (700-790). One of the fundamental Zen texts recited daily in Soto Zen temples in Japan, quoted and commented upon by a number of masters. The Sandôkai ends with the famous line: "You who seek the Way, I beg you, do not waste the present moment."

Sangha, (Jap): (Skrt, *Samgha*). Gathering of monks, but more widely, the community of disciples. One of the "three treasures" of Buddhism alongside the Buddha and the *dharma*.

Sanko, (Jap): Life in the mountains, in the forest, in a quiet place like a *sesshin*, and by extension: not being influenced or absorbed by the environment, including the environment of others.

Sanpai, (Jap): A series of three prostrations, with the forehead touching the ground and the palms of the hands lifting upwards.

Satori, (Jap): Enlightenment or awakening. Not a special state of consciousness, but a returning to the normal condition, to one's original nature. In the Rinzai School *satori* is the end result of fruitful practice and is the object of a fierce quest. In the Soto school, practice itself is *satori* meaning the actualization of our true nature.

Sawaki, Kodo, 1880-1965: Great Japanese Soto Master and master of Taisen Deshimaru. Ordained by Sawada Koho when he was eighteen years old, he studied closely with Master Shokoku Zenko. He spent the greater part of his life outside temples, travelling around Japan, to spread the practice of zazen, which earned him the nickname of "Homeless Kodo."

Sekito, (Jap): (Ch. Che-t'e or Si-k'ien), 700-790. "Stone Head." Disciple of Seigen and Master of Yakusan. Considered the first link in the Soto Zen lineage. Author of the *Sandôkai*, one of the fundamental Soto Zen texts. In the chronicles of the time it was said that, "Baso lived west of the river, Sekito to the south of the lake. Men go from one to the other. Those who have not met them live in ignorance."

Sensei, (Jap): Teacher. In ordinary Japanese language this is a term used by students to address their teachers. In Zen and in the martial arts it is filled with meaning, implying the respect and love which characterizes the relationship between disciple and master. Master Deshimaru preferred to be called this rather than *roshi* which he found pretentious and pompous.

Senzaki, 1876-1958: Ordained a Rinzai monk at the age of nineteen, he left Japan in 1905, accompanying another monk on his mission to the United States. He spent the rest of his life studying, working and teaching Zen in his "floating Dojo." In 1919 he published *101 Zen Tales*. After the attack on Pearl Harbor in 1941 he was imprisoned in Heart Mountain Camp in Wyoming where he stayed till the end of the war. He lived in Los Angeles until his death.

Seppo, (Jap): (Ch. Hsueh-feng I-ts'un), 822-908. Zen master, disciple of Tokusan and master of Gensha and Unmon. When he was 17, he shut himself away in a cave where Master Reikun had lived. By the time he was 54, he had founded his own temple on a steep mountain attracting thousands of monks.

Sesshin, (Jap): "To touch the mind." A period of communal retreat lasting several days, dedicated to the intensive practice of zazen, interspersed with *samu*.

Shakyamuni, (Skrt): "The Sage of the Shakya." The historical Buddha.

Shiho, (Jap): The transmission of the *dharma* which traditionally happens at midnight between master and disciple, so authenticating the latter as one of the successors of Buddha in the lineage concerned.

Shiki, (Jap): Phenomena or consciousness of the phenomenal world. *Shiki sokuze ku, ku sokuze shiki*; phenomena become (are) emptiness, emptiness becomes (is) phenomena. Form is emptiness, Emptiness is form.

Shin Jin Mei, (Jap): "The Poem of Faith in Mind" by Master Sosan, the third Patriarch. Composed in the 7th Century AD it is one of the oldest *Ch'an* texts transmitted in Zen. It affirms the faith in mind when all dualistic standpoints have been abandoned.

Shinran, (Jap), 1172-1262: Founder of the Japanese Buddhist School *Jodo-shin-shu,* "The true school of the Pure Land," or *Shin* school. The essential doctrine of the *Jodo-shin-shu* is contained within a formula for the adoration of Amida (*nembutsu*) in whom all the virtues of Buddha are contained. The recitation of this formula allows the faithful to be reborn in the pure land of Amida and to realize Buddhahood, even if they have a bad karma.

Shobogenzo, (Jap): "The Treasury-eye of the True Way" traditionally designates the teaching transmitted by Buddha outside of texts. In Soto Zen it refers to a masterwork by Master Dogen, partly compiled by his disciple Ejo. Prof. Takahashi, however, translates the title of this monumental teaching, thus: "The right teaching concerning the true and essential spirit of Buddhism." And Master Deshimaru translates it thus: "The treasury of the highest truth, the mind of Buddha." (*See* "The voice of the Valley" for more on this title). The *Shobogenzo* is the first great Buddhist writing in Japanese. A dense text of inexhaustible richness which recapitulates and develops all the teachings received in China by the founder of Soto Zen in Japan. Not content to "follow the footsteps of the ancient masters," Dogen elaborated on the traditional themes with great freedom and impressive virtuosity.

Shuso, (Jap): Assistant to the master during zazen or in a *sesshin*. It is his or her task to oversee the smooth running of the dojo. The *shuso* is responsible for the harmony in the dojo and all that happens there: the practitioners' postures, the responsibilities of the *kyosaku*, of the drum and the bells, the pillars, the ceremony, etc.

Sojiji, (Jap): One of the two principal temples of Soto Zen in Japan, founded by Master Keizan.

Sokei-an, 1882-1945: Rinzai Zen master, one of the first to settle in the United States. He founded The Buddhist Society of America in 1930, known today as the First Zen Institute of America. During the Second World War he was imprisoned in Maryland in 1942, and like Master Senzaki, himself imprisoned in Wyoming, they were declared by the government as "Foreign enemy." Sokei-an was let out in 1943 and died two years later without having appointed a successor.

Sotoshu, (Soto school): School founded in China in the 9th century by Master Tozan (Ch. Tung-shan Liang-chieh) and his disciple Sozan (Ch. Ts'ao-shan Pen-chi). Also called the "Zen of Silent Illumination" as opposed to the "Zen of the Contemplation of words" (Rinzai). Soto was introduced to Japan by Dogen in 1227 when he returned from China. Three generations later the school had developed into two branches, Eihei-ji and Soji-ji. In any case, in the Soto school zazen is practiced facing the wall without object or goal.

Suchness: (Skrt. *tathata*. Jap. *inmo*) "Things as they are." Authentic nature, unconditioned by anything.

Sumeru, (Skrt). Name given to the mountain situated in the middle of the earth in Buddhist cosmology; it is also the axis of the sun's and moon's revolutions. It rests upon a vast ocean and is surrounded by chains of mountains and seas. The Buddhist concept of Sumeru represents the vision of an enlightened being, *arhat* or Buddha. Thanks to the "divine eye," the birth and death of the universe, all beings therein, and the states in which they are reborn, can be seen.

Sutra, (Skrt): (Jap, *kyo* or *gyo,*). Sermons given by Buddha. According to tradition, they were memorized and pronounced at the First Buddhist Council in 480 BCE, by his disciple Ananda, shortly after Shakyamuni's death. They generally begin with the words, "Such as I have heard." Although the Hinayana sutras (tripitaka) have come to us in their Pali or Sanskrit versions, the Mahayana sutras are known for the most part in their Tibetan or Chinese translation.

Suzuki, D.T: (1870-1966). Buddhist erudite, translator and propagator of Zen in the West. Adept of the *koan* method. He studied Zen according to Shaku Soen and Sokatsu Shaku who gave him the task of translating the Zen texts into English for public knowledge.

Suzuki, Shunryu, (1904-1971): Monk of the Soto Zen School, he studied at the Buddhist University of Komazawa and then in the temples of Eihei-ji and Soji-ji. In 1958, aged 53 and already a deeply respected Zen master in Japan, Shunryu Suzuki left for the United States and settled in San Francisco. Under his direction seven centers of Soto Zen Buddhist practice opened in America, of which one was the Zen Mountain Center, the first Zen temple outside of Asia.

Takuan, (1573-1645): Rinzai Zen Master of the Tokugawa period whose teaching had a strong influence on the art of combat (*bujutsu*). He was the master of the samurai Miyamoto Musashi.

Taoism: Mystic doctrine centered on the Tao, the original, primordial and immutable principle, in other words "the Way," *wu-wei*, non-action. Taoism is a philosophy and at the same time a Chinese religion. Testified to since the end of the 4th century BCE, an era in which Lao Tsu's *Tao Te Ching* was composed. This version of Taoism delves into the roots of shamanic thought of prehistoric China. It expresses in its practices—amongst other rituals, medicinal, physical and culinary—a harmonious vision between the human and the environment. It had a great influence on all the Far East and on Zen in particular.

Tokusan, (Jap): (Ch. Te-shan Hsuan-chien), 781-867. Disciple of Ryutan and master of Seppo. Erudite known for his knowledge of the Diamond Sutra, he burnt all his books to follow the Way and dedicate himself to the practice of zazen. Well known for his method of education named *bokatsu* (from *bo*, "stick" and *katsu*, "shout").

Tôzan, (Jap): (Ch.ung-shan Liang-chieh) 807-869. Disciple of Ungan (780-841) and master of Ungo (?-902) amongst others. With Sozan (840-901) he was the founder of the Soto Zen school. Author of the *Hokyo Zanmai* (*Samadhi of the Precious Mirror*) one of the fundamental Zen texts. This text is recited in Japanese temples.

Uji: "Being time." One of the chapters of the *Shobogenzo* written by Master Dogen in 1240, in which the accent is placed upon the interpenetration between "being" and "time." One cannot stand up without the other since they mutually affirm one another.

Unmon, (Jap): (Ch. Yün-men Wen-yen), 864-949. Zen master, disciple and successor of Seppo. He founded a school which died out in the 12th century. His responses and quotations play a great part in Zen tradition. He is notably the author of the phrase: "Every day is a good day." Up until the Cultural Revolution in China, his mummified body sitting in the posture of zazen could be viewed in the Yunmen Temple.

Unsui, (Jap): Literally "water-cloud." A term used to describe a Zen monk, who, like the clouds and the water in the river, does not attach themselves to anything.

Upanishad, (Skrt): Sacred Hindu texts which together form the Vedanta (there are more than 200). Many are recent, but some date back to a very ancient time, between 700 and 300 BCE. Their aim is to free people from transmigration.

Vajrayana, (Skrt): "the way of the diamond." This term corresponds to tantric Buddhism which was developed in India between the 6th and 11th centuries and then spread to Nepal and Tibet, particularly after the arrival of Atisha in 1042. Vajrayana Buddhism gave birth to several sects which called on the practices of tantra and yoga to attain enlightenment.

Vedas, (Skrt): The most ancient religious texts in the world rewritten by the Indo-Aryan community. Transcriptions of oral teachings transmitted from brahmin to brahmin since the 16th century BCE, they constitute the main body of reference for all Hindus.

Vimalakirti, (Skrt): Lay disciple of Buddha whose understanding surpasses that of monks. According to the text of the Great Vehicle which carries his name, Vimalakirti was of an incredible erudition.

Way: (*tao* or *do* in Chinese). The cosmic order, or the path. The practice in harmony with the cosmic order. The Way of Buddha: *butsu-do*.

Zafu: Round cushion filled with kapok upon which one sits for the practice of zazen. A replica of the herbal cushion upon which Shakyamuni attained *satori*.

Zanshin, (Jap): An attitude of concentration of the mind in the martial arts. After having placed a strike, practitioners should not let their attention go, lest they fail to come through again with another attack. It is the mind which continues *after* the action, which is important.

Zaso, (Jap): Another word for zazen.

Zazen, (Jap): (Ch, *T'so chan*). *Za* means "to be seated." In Soto practice, it is to sit cross-legged, in a lotus or half-lotus posture on a *zafu*, facing the wall.

Zazenshin: "the Needle of Zazen" Poem about the meaning of zazen, the essence of the *dharma*, written by Wanshi Shogaku in the 12th century, then commented upon and reworked by Master Dogen in the *Shobogenzo*.

Zen, (Jap): Abbreviation of the word *zenna*, a Japanese transcript of the Chinese term, *chan'na* which comes from the Sanskrit *dhyana*. It means concentration of the mind, attention. Branch of Mahayana Buddhism, introduced into Japan by the masters Eisai and Dogen in the 13th century.

Zeisler, Étienne Mokusho. (Fr. 1943-1990). A close disciple and interpreter of Master Deshimaru.

Zuimonki, (Jap): Or *Shobogenzo Zuimonki*. Collection of Master Dogen's teachings which arose out of instruction and conversations with his disciples, compiled by his assistant and successor Ejo (1198-1280). The *Zuimonki* is mainly about the moral rules of behavior in everyday life.

ABOUT THE AUTHOR

Philippe Rei Ryu Coupey was born and grew up in New York. After his studies in literature, he took up several odd jobs which were as improbable as they were formative, notably uranium prospector, building painter, social secretary, translator, and security guard, among others.

In 1969, Coupey moved to Paris where he happened to meet the Zen master Taisen Deshimaru just outside his residence. He became a very close disciple of Deshimaru, working on his teachings which were given in English. As a result of this collaboration, three books were published.

Ordained as a monk, he followed his master until Deshimaru's death in 1982. Since then, he has continued to practice and teach in the International Zen Association (AZI). With his disciples, Coupey perpetuates the tradition of monks without residency: to live their lives in society and come together to practice in different places of temporary usage. Advisor to thirty Zen groups in France, Germany, and Switzerland, Coupey facilitates numerous exchanges between French practitioners and those from other countries.

Today Coupey lives and practices in Paris. Many of his disciples have begun to teach in their own right.

Contact Information: ohnebleibe@gmail.com

ABOUT HOHM PRESS

Hohm Press is committed to publishing books that provide readers with alternatives to the materialistic values of the current culture, and promote self-awareness, the recognition of interdependence, and compassion. Our subject areas include parenting, transpersonal psychology, religious studies, women's studies, the arts and poetry.

Contact Information: Hohm Press, PO Box 4410, Chino Valley, Arizona, 86323, USA; 800-381-2700, or 928-636-3331; email: publisher@hohmpress.com